SECOND EDITION

Powerful Lesson Planning

To Raymond—for his support, enthusiasm, advice, and friendly criticism

Janice Skowron

SECOND EDITION

Powerful Lesson Planning

Every Teacher's Guide to Effective Instruction

Foreword by Charlotte Danielson

CORWIN PRESS
A SAGE Publications Company
Thousand Oaks, California

For information:

Corwin Press
A Sage Publications Company
2455 Teller Road
Thousand Oaks, California 91320
www.corwinpress.com

Sage Publications Ltd.
1 Oliver's Yard
55 City Road
London EC1Y 1SP
United Kingdom

Sage Publications India Pvt. Ltd.
B-42, Panchsheel Enclave
Post Box 4109
New Delhi 110 017 India

Printed in the United States of America.

Library of Congress Cataloging-in-Publication Data

Skowron, Janice.
Powerful lesson planning: Every teacher's guide to effective
instruction / Janice Skowron.— 2nd ed.
    p. cm.
Rev. ed. of: Powerful lesson planning models, ©2001.
Includes bibliographical references and index.
ISBN 1-4129-3730-2 (cloth) — ISBN 1-4129-3731-0 (pbk.)
    1. Instructional systems—Design. 2. Lesson planning. 3. Effective teaching. I. Skowron, Janice. Powerful lesson planning models. II. Title.
LB1028.38.S56 2006
371.3'028—dc22   2005037827

This book is printed on acid-free paper.

06 07 08 09 10 9 8 7 6 5 4 3 2 1

Acquisitions Editor:	Cathy Hernandez
Editorial Assistant:	Charline Wu
Production Editor:	Diane S. Foster
Copy Editor:	Robert Holm
Typesetter:	C&M Digitals (P) Ltd.
Proofreader:	Scott Oney
Indexer:	Molly Hall

Contents

Reproducible
Pages Directory

Foreword

*P*owerful Lesson Planning: Every Teacher's Guide to Effective Instruction is an important book, offering teachers essential guidance in the highly complex task of lesson planning. It provides four models: basic, integrated, differentiated, and problem-based. These models are progressively more complex and nuanced, providing teachers with guidance as they increase their lesson planning proficiency.

As I set forth in *Enhancing Professional Practice: A Framework for Teaching*, planning is one of the four essential domains of professional practice (Danielson, 1996). Further, planning is, of course, highly cerebral, requiring high-level thinking and decision making. And in this age of content standards and the high-stakes assessments of those standards, the teacher's challenge in planning for instruction is more profound than ever.

Textbooks and other instructional materials provide teachers with learning objectives, activities, assessments, and of course, materials needed—all they need for instructional planning. Teachers have the option, if they so choose, to simply follow the directions and "connect the dots." In many cases, the instructional suggestions offered by the textbooks and ancillary materials are as viable as those that many teachers (particularly novices) could create on their own. However, only teachers know their own students (and therefore how to differentiate instruction to assist them), and content standards are different in different locations. Therefore, if teachers can acquire sophisticated planning skills, they will be able to offer a richer instructional environment for their students than if they relied solely on their text materials.

Powerful Lesson Planning: Every Teacher's Guide to Effective Instruction works equally well for novice teachers and for seasoned professionals. The beginner will likely feel most comfortable with the basic model. With enough practice, this model becomes perfected to the extent that it can be built upon. The models described subsequently (integrated, differentiated, and problem-based) are advanced, requiring skills rarely demonstrated by those just entering the profession. The skills and practice needed to successfully implement these models are highly advanced, reflecting a sophisticated level of planning.

Therefore, by mastering the ideas presented in *Powerful Lesson Planning: Every Teacher's Guide to Effective Instruction*, teachers can advance their practice and demonstrate skills I have identified as "proficient" and "distinguished" (Danielson, 1996). And if teachers can develop these skills in collaboration with their colleagues, their professional experience will be doubly rewarding.

—Charlotte Danielson
Author and Educational Consultant

Preface

Do you remember your first teaching assignment—the first day you entered your new classroom and thought about the students who would soon be there? For me, it was a combination of pride and anxiety. I was proud that I had finally attained what I had prepared for over the last several years. I was also extremely anxious about the first day with my students. What would they be like? Would they like me? And most important, how could I best teach them? Sure, I had been in classrooms before. I had planned and taught lessons. But this was different. This was no short-term assignment with someone to guide me along the way. I was on my own. I had signed the contract, and I was expected to be a professional.

The first few days of my teaching assignment, I was overwhelmed with information about school rules and regulations, extracurricular assignments, curriculum requirements, and schedules. A kindly colleague offered the advice to "always have something for them to do." So I studied all the curriculum guides and teachers' manuals (I had never seen them before!). I made sure I had enough worksheets. I decorated my classroom with bulletin boards and attractive displays. I worked from dawn to midnight for weeks to get ready for the first day. When it arrived, I was exhausted. Somehow my students and I survived that day—I'm sure I learned more than they did. What I learned was that I needed a plan. If I was going to be any good at all at this teaching thing (and I desperately wanted to be), I was the one who had to make it happen. Certainly I could make sure I always had something for them to do, but I wanted to make sure I always had something for them to learn.

It is interesting the way competence and confidence go hand in hand. After several years, I felt more competent and at ease—but I was still very much a beginning teacher. As I came to know more about how learning happens, I tried different instructional designs. I put several objectives into the same lesson; I tailored lessons for different students; I let students take the lead, not only in what they learned but in how they learned. There were successes, but there were also disappointments. Not everything worked. But my teaching evolved and my students progressed.

Looking back over my early teaching years, I wish I had had more guidance. I read professional journals and learned a great deal about theory and philosophy, what to do and what not to do. But there was very little on how to actually do it. I wish there had been some models I could have used rather than trying to reinvent the wheel; it would have made teaching easier. I did not realize it then, but this is where the ideas for *Powerful Lesson Planning* models took root.

Over the years, I have played many roles in education—classroom teacher, reading specialist, administrator, university professor, and consultant. As I listen to and talk with classroom teachers from kindergarten through high school and in graduate programs and school districts throughout the country, I am taken back to my early experiences as a classroom teacher. I listen as teachers express their concerns and frustrations as well as their joys and desires about teaching. In very candid moments, when expressions of doubt sometimes surface, teachers question their practices. Many realize that the approaches they have used for many years no longer work as well as they once did. Their students have changed—and they have changed. Many are willing to try new approaches but simply don't know how to go about it. So, for lack of information, they go on doing what they've always done. As one veteran teacher said, "This year we're supposed to differentiate. We had a big meeting where we heard why it's a good idea. But no one told us how to do it. We're left on our own."

Not surprisingly, even experienced teachers who are familiar with basic instructional design may find it difficult to implement more complex instructional approaches. The planning procedures for different approaches involve asking different questions and making different decisions. Experienced teachers, regardless of content area or grade level, need models as they plan more complex instructional designs. Models provide a focus and common language for discussion and understanding.

Learning to plan effective lessons is part of the preparatory coursework in teacher education programs. Preclinical and student teaching experiences provide opportunities for the preservice teacher to observe and discuss lesson plans with experienced practitioners. Initially, preservice and beginning teachers focus on a very basic form of lesson planning that includes defining the learning standards to be achieved, selecting the activities to facilitate learning to meet the standard, and developing an appropriate assessment of student learning. At this stage, practicing more complex planning for diverse classrooms is not the norm (Tomlinson et al., 1997). Unless basic instructional design is understood and practiced, there can be little understanding of how to plan more complex instructional designs. With proficiency in basic instructional design, the beginning teacher is ready to expand and refine his or her teaching. Without this proficiency, the beginning teacher is likely to be confused and bewildered when trying to design something more complex.

Approximately 40 percent of teachers in the United States plan to retire by 2010. The National Center for Education Statistics (2005) predicts that the demand for teachers will continue and increase over the next five years as large numbers of teachers retire and student enrollments increase. Many students will be taught by novice teachers, many of whom will come to teaching through alternative paths.

Individuals who have content expertise do not always have the pedagogical expertise to design effective instruction. Their effectiveness depends on their ability to analyze content information, skills, and processes in terms of how to teach. An Instructional Design Planning Guide provides a tool for these teachers to connect content to instruction. An instructional plan sets the stage for teaching and learning. It is the blueprint for instruction.

An instructional plan documents what and how students will learn. The purpose of *Powerful Lesson Planning* is to bring into focus the decisions teachers face as they plan instruction. In this book, teachers are guided through four major instructional designs: basic, integrated, differentiated, and problem-based.

Instructional design is a thinking process that results in a product—the instructional plan. *Powerful Lesson Planning* provides a series of key questions and a step-by-step process for developing instructional plans. The instructional plan emerges as the teacher contemplates key questions and makes decisions related to them. This structured step-by-step process is used as a starting point. Modifications to fit individual circumstances may be made once the process is fully understood. Descriptive information and instructional design tools—key questions, outlines, templates, and examples—are provided to facilitate the planning process.

OVERVIEW OF THE INSTRUCTIONAL DESIGN PROCESS

Powerful Lesson Planning provides Instructional Design Planning Guides composed of key questions for planning each of the four instructional designs. Each Instructional Design Planning Guide includes three sections: Section 1: Desired Results—Standards and Performance Descriptors; Section 2: Assessment—Evidence of Learning; and Section 3: Lesson Design. The planning process begins with the teacher focusing on the key questions and making decisions related to what students will learn and how that learning will occur. This process produces the "data" the teacher uses to construct more specific learning plans. While the process of using the Instructional Design Planning Guide and completing the instructional design form is generally the same for each of the four models, the key questions differ, and planning tools are specific to each particular model.

Common to all the instructional designs is the lesson plan that documents the learning standards, assessments, teaching strategies, and learning activities. When teachers practice and perfect their skill in planning a basic lesson, they are able to design more complex approaches to learning.

The chapters in *Powerful Lesson Planning* cover each instructional model: basic, integrated, differentiated, and problem-based. A brief description of each chapter follows.

Chapter 1: Basic Instructional Design

This chapter begins with a discussion of the importance of planning as it relates to expert teaching. The development of intuitive teaching is explained as the result of the teacher's learning, experience, practice, and reflection.

Chapter 1 describes a basic planning structure for teaching specific learning standards. While learning standards may differ somewhat from state to state, the design process presented in this chapter may be used in any standards-led system. The planning process is made clear through the use of planning templates, models, illustrations, and graphics.

Preservice and novice teachers can use the basic instructional design model to gain experience in lesson planning. The following are the tools used to develop a basic lesson plan:

1. The Basic Instructional Design Planning Guide, with suggested planning resources, notes, and comments, meant to assist the teacher in responding to important questions related to lesson planning

2. The Basic Instructional Design Preliminary Planning form to be completed by the teacher as a planning worksheet

3. An example of a completed Basic Instructional Design Planning Guide

4. Basic Lesson Plan form

5. Two sample completed lesson plans

Chapter 2: Integrated Instructional Design

Integrating learning standards from various content areas in meaningful ways for students is the focus of Chapter 2. It begins with the rationale and research that support integrated learning. The Integrated Instructional Design Planning Guide is provided to facilitate the planning process. The tools used to develop an Integrated Instructional Design Plan are summarized below:

1. The Integrated Instructional Design Planning Guide, with suggested planning resources, notes, and comments, meant to assist the teacher in responding to the guiding questions and completing the Integrated Instructional Design Plan

2. The Integrated Instructional Planning Questions and Decisions form to be completed by the teacher as a planning worksheet

3. An example of a completed Integrated Instructional Design Plan

4. Curriculum map examples

5. Integrated Instruction: Overview of Learning Standards form

6. Integrated Instruction Plan form

The Integrated Instructional Design Plan includes the development of a curriculum map—an overview of the topics and concepts studied in each of the curriculum areas. These topics are translated into learning standards on the Integrated Instruction Planner: Overview of Learning Standards form under a major learning theme or "big idea." A teaching overview plan based on the learning standards is developed using the Integrated Instruction Plan form. Specific lesson plans for classroom implementation are developed from this overview.

The instructional design produced in this manner may incorporate many learning standards across the curriculum or focus on a limited number. Planning templates and models throughout the chapter, along with illustrations and graphics, make the planning process manageable and user-friendly.

Chapter 3: Differentiated Instructional Design

Chapter 3 explains how to accommodate and provide successful learning experiences for students of varying levels of abilities, backgrounds, and learning preferences. It discusses the theory, research, and best practices information associated with differentiation. This chapter enables teachers to understand why it is important to differentiate instruction and how to go about doing so.

The differentiated instructional design model differentiates learning activities but holds learning standards constant. Student needs and task demands are the basis for differentiation. The tools used to develop a Differentiated Instructional Design Plan are summarized below:

1. The Differentiated Instructional Design Planning Guide, with suggested planning resources, notes, and comments, meant to assist the teacher in responding to the guiding questions and completing the Differentiated Instructional Design Plan

2. The Differentiated Instructional Design: Planning Questions and Decisions form to be completed by the teacher

3. An example of a completed Differentiated Instructional Design Plan

4. The Differentiated Activities Planning Matrix

The Differentiated Instructional Design: Planning Questions and Decisions form is used as a planning document. The information produced from this form is used to develop a matrix showing the criteria for student differentiation in relation to the learning standards to be taught. Corresponding instructional activities are then developed for each cell in the matrix. Separate minilessons may be developed from this matrix depending on the needs of the students.

Chapter 4: Problem-Based Learning Instructional Design

Problem-based learning is organized around a real-life problem in which students take the lead in determining how to go about solving the problem and working though to a resolution. The teacher is a facilitator in the process—offering resources, coaching, monitoring, and conducting minilessons. Chapter 4 is an introductory, straightforward explanation of problem-based learning—how it originated, how to develop problem statements, and how to incorporate standards and assessment into problem-based activities. A discussion of the teacher's role in problem-based learning illustrates the planning perspective required in this approach. The chapter covers the importance and use of technology resources and provides sample Web sites.

Problem-based learning appears complex, but teachers may use a variety of planning strategies to make this approach manageable. The thinking process questions provided in Chapter 4 help teachers sort out and see the total picture, even if the details must be filled in later. It is recommended that this instructional design be undertaken after the teacher has had some experience with integrated and differentiated instructional designs.

The tools used to develop a Problem-Based Instructional Design Plan are summarized below:

1. The Problem-Based Learning Planning Guide, with suggested planning resources, notes, and comments, meant to assist the teacher in responding to the guiding questions and completing the Problem-Based Instructional Design Plan

2. The Problem-Based Learning Instructional Design: Planning Questions and Decisions form to be completed by the teacher as a planning worksheet

3. An example of a completed Problem-Based Learning Planning Guide

4. Problem-Based Learning Standards Overview

5. Problem-Based Learning Assessment Planner

Resources

The Resources section contains a discussion of professional teaching standards, both for beginning teachers and accomplished teachers. It also contains the student evaluation standards and Web sites of professional organizations.

HOW TO USE THIS BOOK

Preservice and novice teachers will find it helpful to become thoroughly familiar with basic lesson design as presented in Chapter 1. A firm grounding in the basics helps to ensure success in using more complex models. After teachers become confident in planning basic instruction, they may mentally review or modify the Basic Instructional Design Planning Guide. It is probably not necessary to write out responses to the key questions once the planning process is well known.

Even experienced teachers benefit from having a structure to guide instructional planning. However, the planning process for these teachers is somewhat different in that their background knowledge enables them to take some short-cuts and make some modifications. Flexibility is built into the planning templates to accommodate a wide range of teaching experience. Experienced teachers may wish to review the Instructional Design Planning Guide to remind themselves of information they already have and tap into their prior knowledge related to instructional planning.

Teachers who have used a single content area approach to planning and teaching and are ready to try integrated, differentiated, or problem-based instructional designs benefit from going through the entire thinking process using the Instructional Design Planning Guides. This facilitates in-depth understanding and makes subsequent planning more efficient. It is hoped that *Powerful Lesson Planning* will help teachers to revitalize current practices, expand their repertoire of approaches, and improve learning for students.

Powerful Lesson Planning, second edition, contains the same organizational format that made the first edition so popular with teachers. Sections relating to assessment have been expanded to allow more in-depth information as it relates to student learning, and new examples show how lesson planning looks at different grade levels.

This book is for those teachers who are at the beginning of their teaching careers and for those who desire to make better classrooms for students through thoughtful planning. It is what I would have wanted those many years ago when I first stepped into a classroom. This jump-start of a book makes no assumptions of prior knowledge. It covers the basics of lesson planning, integrated instruction, differentiated instruction, and problem-based learning. Specific examples of planning guides for these approaches serve as models for teachers to form and fit their own ideas into new ways of teaching.

Publisher's Acknowledgments

Corwin Press gratefully acknowledges the contributions of the following reviewers:

Diane Boarman, Middle School Science Teacher
Howard County Public Schools, MD

Stacey Edmonson, Associate Professor of Educational Leadership
Sam Houston State University, Huntsville, TX

Tonia M. Guidry, Eighth Grade Math Teacher
Golden Meadow Middle School, Golden Meadow, LA

Rachel Hull, Fourth Grade Teacher
Buffalo Elementary School, Buffalo, WV

Mark Johnson, Fifth Grade Teacher
Windy Hills Elementary School, Kearney, NE

Faith Kline, Curriculum Coordinator
Wailupe Valley Elementary School, Honolulu, HI

Valdine McLean, Chemistry, Biology, and Physics Teacher
Pershing County High School, Lovelock, NV

About the Author

 **Janice Skowron,** EdD, is a highly regarded educational consultant known for facilitating interactive, engaging workshops for teachers and administrators on curriculum and instructional planning in reading and the language arts. Using research-proven strategies, she models and shows teachers how to create effective lessons for basic, integrated, differentiated, and problem-based learning. She has experience as a classroom teacher, reading specialist, university instructor, and school and district administrator at the elementary and middle school levels. She is a frequent presenter at professional conferences and has authored numerous educational materials and articles.

Basic Instructional Design

I t is not difficult to recognize classrooms that are alive with purposeful activity and exude a feeling that "there's important work going on here." Students are engaged in their work. They understand the direction and importance of their activity. The teacher is a facilitator—coaching, questioning, and providing resources for students at opportune times. There is an atmosphere of authenticity that resembles real life. Independence is balanced with interdependence as a means to learning. Some of the time, students learn with others in small groups, some of the time they work independently, and at other times they are part of whole-class activity. Such a classroom does not just happen. It is the result of careful and precise planning by the teacher.

The difference is in the details . . .

Nor is it difficult to recognize classrooms where learning has little direction or focus. Students are off task and lack a sense of purpose. They appear to be disinterested and bored with activities that hold little challenge. They neither understand the purpose of their work nor believe in its importance. Though the teacher may have good intentions, he or she has not created the foundation necessary for effective learning. There is little evidence of careful and precise planning for instruction.

A critical difference between these classrooms is the underlying plan that details what students will learn and how they will learn it. A well-functioning classroom is based on a well-designed plan. According to Costa and Garmston (1994, p. 90), "Planning may well include the most important decisions teachers make because it is the phase upon which all other decisions rest." Good planning sets the stage for good teaching, which in turn fosters optimal learning. Teachers who know how to plan know precisely what they want to accomplish—or more exactly, what they want their students to accomplish. Poor planning results in no one, including the teacher, having a clear understanding of what is to be accomplished. Effective instruction starts with an organized instructional plan.

FROM HERE TO INTUITIVE TEACHING

Some teachers appear to be intuitive. They facilitate student learning with ease and agility. They are confident, insightful, and expert. They not only know the standards that constitute accomplished teaching but also are able to translate the standards into effective instruction. Becoming an exceptional teacher is a learning process that some believe never ends. The teacher is in a continual state of learning, building, and refining teaching practices. A theoretical model of the complex nature of exceptional teaching is shown in Figure 1.1. The outermost layer represents expert teaching actions and behaviors. It is where ease and competence are exhibited—where actions appear to be intuitive. It is easy to observe the effortless actions of teaching in the intuitive layer, but there is much more than meets the eye. Other layers, hidden from view, are powerful determiners of the outer layer.

At the core of the model in Figure 1.1 is the teacher's mental schema for teaching. It is an amalgam of all the information, concepts, skills, processes, attitudes, values, and beliefs the teacher holds regarding teaching. The second layer shows the interaction of metacognition, reflection, practice, and experience. This interaction impacts and changes the schema. The third layer is automaticity. *Automaticity* is behavior that develops through a multitude of repetitions; knowing how to do something and then engaging in repetitive practice. Such behaviors may be mental or physical (Samuels, 1994). Driving a car is an example of automaticity. The inexperienced driver consciously refers to mental notes regarding the physical act of turning the steering wheel and coordinating this with gas pedal pressure, all while visually judging distance to

Teaching expertise develops through the interaction of metacognition, reflection, practice, and experience.

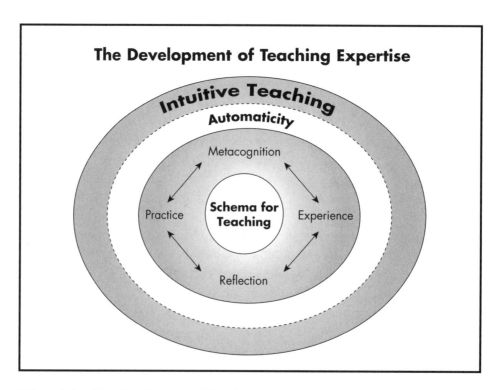

Figure 1.1 The Development of Teaching Expertise

remain in the appropriate lane and not impact the vehicle directly ahead. The experienced driver, on the other hand, turns the vehicle with effortless ease—with no apparent conscious thought given to the task. Driving the car has become automatic. In much the same manner, teaching becomes automatic.

The outermost layer of the illustration is intuitive teaching—the quick, effortless, competent action observed in exceptional teachers. Exceptional teachers combine automaticity and metacognition. They constantly assess the teaching-learning process, know when it is going well, know when to change something, and have a vast repertoire of automatic responses that may be brought into play. Developing this outer layer is a complex process that happens over time and is unique to each teacher.

Now, imagine the two-dimensional image in Figure 1.1 as a three-dimensional sphere made of clear plastic. Imagine the layers within the sphere separated by permeable membranes through which thoughts, ideas, learning, attitudes, beliefs, skills, and knowledge flow freely. Imagine that only the outermost layer of the sphere is observable to others. Those who observe the sphere see only the expert in action. Those who understand the complexity of teaching understand the knowledge, skills, processes, and multitude of experiences that shape the outermost layer.

EXPERIENCE AND PRACTICE

Experience is the heart of know-how, as in the expression: "He has real know-how." Know-how does not just happen. It develops through experience and exposure to new ideas, methods, and strategies. It develops as the teacher thinks and reflects on the meaning of the experiences and fits new information into his or her pattern of knowledge. "Professional knowledge is seen as coming both from sources outside the teacher and from the teachers' own interpretations of their everyday experiences" (Sparks-Langer & Colton, 1991, p. 37). Obviously, without exposure to new ideas and ways of doing things, teachers will continue for better or worse with their present practices.

Effective teachers plan precisely and comprehensively.

The opportunity to learn new things is critical if teachers are to grow professionally. Professional development programs are one source of knowledge input. But not all things "learned" through professional development will be retained or used. Knowledge must be transferred and applied in real teaching situations. According to Bellanca (1995), effective professional development experiences are consistent with constructivist theory:

> Constructivist theoreticians view learning transfer as the most complex and important element in the learning process. Without transfer either by hugging (an immediate connection within the curriculum) or bridging (a wider connection across the curriculum or into life), learning is incomplete. Thus, transfer cannot be an instructional afterthought or something that just "happens." It must be a consciously planned result of taking something (a skill, idea, concept, value, etc.) and moving it somewhere (across a lesson, unit, course, job, etc.) by means of a carefully selected somehow. (p. 18)

Effective teachers plan precisely and comprehensively. They have a clear picture of what they wish to accomplish and how they will go about doing it. They practice the elements of planning and teaching over and over, eventually reaching a point at which the elements and actions are internalized, allowing greater ease of use. But practice alone does not ensure improvement. New learning combined with metacognition and reflection contributes to effective practice.

When teachers plan instruction, they engage in a complex mental process. In the beginning, the process is conscious and deliberate. The novice teacher applies a great deal of thought to planning instruction. Every component, every step of the instructional plan is thought through and written out in detail. The teacher visualizes the enactment of the plan, makes changes, refines, and completes the plan. The experienced teacher, on the other hand, who has used the instructional design components in planning and teaching, has a well-developed schema for instructional planning. He or she plans easily and efficiently and no longer needs to attend to every precise detail. This teacher has reached a level of "knowing" the answers to a myriad of questions and decisions that accompany instructional planning. Deliberate thought is replaced by automatic action (Sparks-Langer & Colton, 1991). Instructional planning has reached a level of automaticity that resembles intuition. However, when questioned regarding the purposes, standards, connections, and approaches used, the accomplished teacher is able to fully explain the various lesson elements.

So, is there such a thing as intuitive teaching? Yes—and no. No if the definition of *intuitive* is instinctive. Yes, in terms of the development of automatic and metacognitive processes. Intuitive teachers are expert planners who understand instructional planning and know how to design instruction. "Intuition" develops through automaticity as teachers use prior knowledge, engage in precision planning, put plans into action, and reflect on the outcome of their instruction.

PROFESSIONAL TEACHING STANDARDS

Danielson's *Enhancing Professional Practice: A Framework for Teaching* (1996) describes 22 components of teaching divided into four major domains: planning and preparation, classroom environment, instruction, and professional responsibilities. According to Danielson, this framework provides a road map for novice teachers and guidance for experienced teachers. Further, it may be used as a structure for focusing improvement efforts through professional conversation. *And* it communicates to the general public the competencies inherent in teaching.

As one delves into the planning and preparation components in the first domain of Danielson's framework, the multifaceted nature of instructional planning becomes more apparent (Figure 1.2). We can see that the teacher's knowledge and understanding of content (a necessary prerequisite) is by itself not sufficient for effective teaching. Likewise the knowledge and understanding of students is not in itself sufficient for effective teaching. Other components—learning objectives, material resources, instructional strategies, and assessment—are woven into an organized and coherent plan of instruction. Like pieces of a puzzle, all components are necessary to achieve the complete picture.

Like Danielson's domains of teaching, professional standards define teaching for a wide range of audiences within and outside the education profession. Standards document what effective teachers should know and be able to do and provide a common language within which to discuss professional teaching. As important as instructional planning is, it would be a mistake to assume that it is the only component necessary to good teaching. An analysis of what constitutes effective teaching shows the complex interaction of many components. Teaching is far from a simple process. Professional teaching standards describe the important components of effective teaching and direct teachers' efforts toward the

---

Components of Professional Practice

Domain 1: Planning and Preparation

Demonstrating knowledge of content and pedagogy
Knowledge of content
Knowledge of prerequisite relationships
Knowledge of content-related pedagogy

Demonstrating knowledge of students
Knowledge of characteristics of age-group
Knowledge of students' varied approaches to learning
Knowledge of students' skills and knowledge
Knowledge of students' interests and cultural heritage

Selecting instructional goals
Value
Clarity
Suitability for diverse students
Balance

Demonstrating knowledge of resources
Resources for teaching
Resources for students

Designing coherent instruction
Learning activities
Instructional materials and resources
Instructional groups
Lesson and unit structure

Assessing student learning
Congruence with instructional goals
Criteria and standards
Use for planning

SOURCE: From Danielson, C. (1996). *Enhancing Professional Practice: A Framework for Teaching.* Alexandria, VA: ASCD. Used with permission.

Figure 1.2   Components of Professional Practice

---

kind of teaching that makes a difference in the classroom (Darling-Hammond, 1997). It matters greatly that teachers know and apply the professional standards. Standards of the Interstate New Teacher Assessment and Support Consortium (INTASC) and the National Board for Professional Teaching Standards are contained in the Resources section at the end of this book.

DESIGNING POWERFUL LESSONS

The word *design* functions as a verb and a noun. As a verb, *design* is a process that means to draw, plan, or outline. As a noun, *design* is a product, a plan, an arrangement of details. Likewise, *instructional design* is both a process and a product. The teacher "draws" the instructional plan by first determining what learning standards will be taught and then deciding how the standards will be assessed—in other words, (a) what will students learn and (b) what will be the evidence of their learning? Once these decisions are made, the teacher determines appropriate teaching strategies and methods, selects resource and learning materials, and finally, reviews and fine-tunes the entire plan. Instructional design is not a linear process. During the planning phase, decisions are continually adjusted and modified as new ideas and insights present themselves. The final plan reflects the needs and interests of the students for whom it is developed and is a unique reflection of the teacher's style and expertise. The lesson design overview is shown in Figure 1.3.

PLANNING A BASIC LESSON

A basic lesson is one that focuses on a single standard or performance descriptor. It may be a whole-class or small-group lesson. The three major components (or sections—see Figure 1.10) in planning a basic lesson are (1) Desired Results—Standards and Performance Descriptors; (2) Assessment—Evidence of Learning; and (3) Lesson Design. A detailed explanation of each section follows:

Desired Results—Learning Standards and Performance Descriptors

The process of instructional design begins with the learning standards or performance descriptors.

Just as professional teaching standards define teaching practices, learning standards define what students should know and be able to do. Over 50 years ago, Ralph Tyler (1949, p. 45) wrote, "The purpose of a statement of objectives is to indicate the kinds of changes in the student to be brought about so that the instructional activities can be planned and developed in a way likely to attain these objectives; that is, to bring about these changes in students." Tyler's description of learning objectives remains useful in planning instruction based on what students should know and be able to do. Today's terminology of *standards, benchmarks,* and *performance descriptors* may differ from Tyler's terms of *goals* and *objectives,* but his fundamental ideas still hold true. Today all states have developed content learning standards that are meant to give direction in planning instruction and provide the basis for student assessment. An example of a learning standard and its associated performance descriptor for each content area is shown in Figure 1.4. A complete list of learning standards may be found on each state's official Web site. Further information on student learning standards of professional organizations is listed in the Resources section at the end of this book.

The process of instructional design begins with learning standards or performance descriptors. It is this desired end result that drives the planning process and provides the focus and direction for the lesson activities. A clear, precise statement of what students are expected to know and do is the starting point for lesson design (Skowron, 2000). It is important to know that there is a clear distinction and an obvious connection between a learning standard and

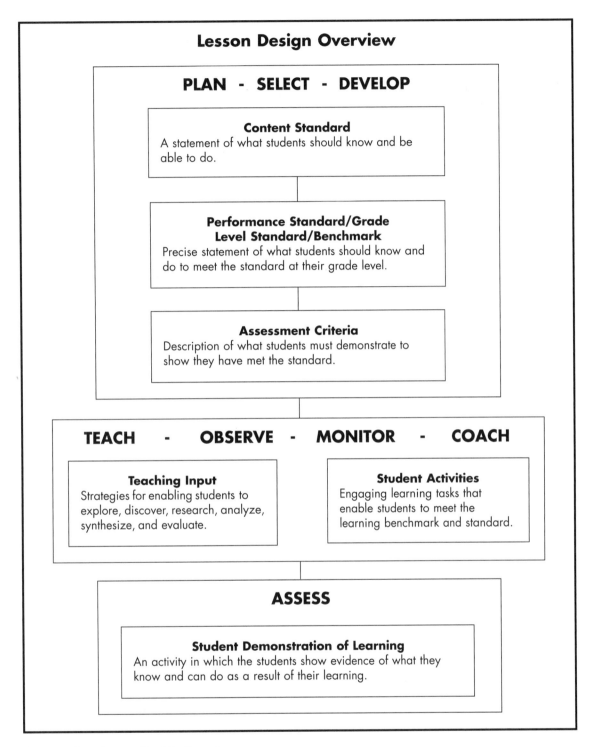

Figure 1.3   Lesson Design Overview

an instructional activity. The *learning standard* clearly states what students should know and do. The *instructional activity* is the vehicle to helping students achieve the standard. It is this desired end result that drives the planning process and provides the focus and direction for the lesson. Wiggins and McTighe (1998) tell us to begin with the end in mind—think first about the desired results.

Content Standards and Performance Descriptors: Examples

Content Area	Learning Standard	Performance Descriptor
Language Arts	Apply reading strategies to improve understanding and fluency.	Identify text structure (description, comparison, cause/effect, sequence) of informational text.
Mathematics	Solve problems using comparison of quantities, ratios, proportions, and percentages.	Create and explain ratios and proportions that represent quantitative relationships.
Social Studies	Understand the development of economic systems.	Describe the impact of trade on the development of early civilizations.
Science	Know and apply concepts that describe how living things interact with each other and with their environment.	Identify survival characteristics of organisms.
Fine Arts	Apply skills and knowledge necessary to create and perform in one or more of the arts.	Sing or play an instrument with expression and accuracy music representing diverse cultures or styles.
Physical Development	Know and apply the principles and components of health-related fitness.	Describe the benefits of maintaining a health-enhancing level of fitness. Participate in physical activity for the purpose of sustaining or improving one's level of fitness.
Foreign Language	Understand oral communication in the target language.	Follow instructions in the target language, given one step at a time, for a wide range of activities.

Figure 1.4   Content Standards and Performance Descriptors: Examples

Assessment—Evidence of Learning

Assessment, or evaluation, is a part of the teaching and learning process. As an evaluative tool, assessment provides information on how well students are progressing toward meeting the standards. As an instructional tool, assessment provides information on student strengths and weaknesses and is used to plan further instruction.

The purpose of assessment is to determine what students have learned in relation to the learning standards. Clear, focused standard statements are targets that lead the way to precise and accurate assessments (Stiggins, Arter, Chappuis, & Chappuis, 2004). For example, if students are expected to write an informational essay that is organized and coherent, then the essay is assessed for organization and coherence. If students are expected to apply correct spelling and grammar in their writing, then their written work is assessed for their ability to apply these conventions. If recall and recognition of information are expected, a multiple-choice or short-answer test would suffice. The link between the standard and assessment should be obvious and understandable. When this is the case, there is no need for additional "test prep." The learning activities themselves are the preparation—and in some cases, may even be the assessment.

Student Evaluation Standards

Assessment must be ethical and concerned for students' well-being. Policies and procedures for assessment should be available to staff, students, parents, and the community. Assessments should be purposeful and useful and provide data that will enhance student learning. The assessments should be practical and nondisruptive by providing information in an efficient manner. And assessments must be accurate; that is, the assessment data should provide sound information that can be analyzed and lead to valid conclusions. Accurate assessments are reliable and valid instruments; they are useful in acquiring data for evaluative and instructional purposes. A reliable assessment yields consistent results. It is free of measurement errors that would distort students' scores. A valid assessment accurately measures what we want it to measure (Popham, 2005). The assessment measures what was taught.

Assessment data should provide sound information that can be analyzed and lead to valid conclusions.

The Student Evaluation Standards: How to Improve Evaluations of Students, developed by the Joint Committee on Standards for Educational Evaluation (2003), categorizes student evaluation standards into four areas:

1. Propriety standards which relate to individual rights and ethical use

2. Utility standards which define use and purpose

3. Feasibility standards which describe practical use

4. Accuracy standards which ensure the use of sound information to produce justifiable conclusions

A summary of *Student Evaluation Standards* is contained in the Resources section at the end of this book.

Types of Assessment

In the broadest sense, assessments may be classified as selected response or performance based. *Selected response assessments* include the pencil-and-paper "traditional" forms of testing (i.e., true-false, multiple choice, short answer). These assessments are useful in determining the student's content knowledge related to facts, information, and processes. *Performance-based assessments* are those that allow students to demonstrate what they can do with the learning they have acquired, such as writing an essay, conducting research, preparing a report, presenting a demonstration, singing, playing a musical instrument, and performing a physical activity. Student performance is assessed with a rubric that accurately and precisely describes the criteria for that performance.

Monitoring Student Progress

Monitoring students as they engage in a learning task is an informal type of assessment and a crucial aspect of teaching. It is important for students to receive feedback on their progress throughout the learning activity. At times encouragement or positive affirmation is all that is needed. At other times clarification or instructional guidance is necessary to prevent misunderstandings. When confused, some students ask for help, but others do not. And still others do not even know they are confused. Monitoring all students is important to obtain diagnostic feedback and determine when intervention through reteaching or additional practice is necessary.

Marzano (2003) endorses the need for effective feedback that is timely and content related. Students benefit when provided with specific comments on what they need to adjust, add, or delete throughout the learning process. Merely indicating right or wrong answers does little to help students improve (Stronge, 2002).

There are several ways to monitor students, ranging from observation in the classroom setting to performance tests and quizzes. Questions that help guide the monitoring process are as follows:

- Does the student exhibit confusion?

- Is the student off task?

- Has the student finished too soon or not soon enough?

- Does the student understand the directions?

- Is there some prior knowledge or prerequisite information the student needs?

- Does the student's response indicate understanding?

It is important for students to receive feedback on their progress throughout the learning activity.

An observation checklist is a tool to monitor student progress during a learning activity. The checklist contains key criteria against which the students are observed (Burke, 2005). The teacher notes the student's performance related to the criteria and indicates whether or not the student meets the criteria. A sample checklist for informational reading at the elementary level appears in Figure 1.5. The checklist helps the teacher determine which students have common difficulties. These students may then be grouped for reteaching, reinforcement, or practice activities.

Another form of student monitoring is through direct questioning on what is being learned. Questioning may be through a verbal exchange between teacher and student or in written form through quizzes, summaries, or reflections. The type of monitoring a teacher chooses to do depends on the demands of the learning situation and the level of complexity and difficulty of the learning standards. Generally, more complex learning is better monitored through direct questioning and observation of performance. Literal learning is more easily monitored through written quizzes and tests.

OBSERVATION CHECKLIST Using Reading Strategies With Nonfiction Text					
• **Formulates predictions**					
• **Verifies predictions**					
• **Formulates questions**					
• **Visualizes text**					
• **Understands descriptions**					
• **Identifies sequence and order**					
• **Compares and contrasts ideas or concepts**					
• **Identifies cause-effect relationships**					
• **States opinions and reasons**					
• **Explains problems and solutions**					
• **Uses inferential thinking**					
• **Connects sources of information**					
• **Self-monitors**					

1 = basic (does not perform without assistance)
2 = developing (performs with some support)
3 = proficient (performs independently)

Figure 1.5   Observation Checklist: Using Reading Strategies With Nonfiction Text

Uses of Assessment

Students want to know how they will be assessed and evaluated. Parents also want to know what their student is learning and how he or she is progressing. Assessment tools such as rubrics and checklists help students and parents understand what is to be learned by pointing out criteria and performance levels (Burke, 2005). When students and parents know the criteria and expectations, student performance often improves.

Assessment in and of itself does not lead to improvement. The real value in assessment data is realized when it is analyzed to determine student strengths and weaknesses and plan further instruction (Gandal & McGiffert, 2003).

Lesson Design

Alignment of learning standards, instructional activities, and assessment ensures that students are assessed on what is taught.

When statements of what is to be learned and how we will measure that learning are in place, instructional activities are planned. *Instructional activities* are what the teacher does to teach the learning standard. The *lesson plan* is a specific and concise outline of what is intended to occur in the lesson. Since assessment is aligned to a learning standard, classroom instruction likewise must be aligned to that standard. Alignment of learning standards, instructional activities, and assessment ensures that students are assessed on what is taught. The components of the lesson plan are described below.

Opening

The opening of the lesson sets the stage for what is to follow. The anticipation that is created motivates students and piques their interest (Hunter, 1984). An effective opening activates students' schemata by tapping into their prior knowledge and making connections to new learning. Calling to mind what is already known is critical for learning. Jensen (2000) says that the more associations and connections one makes, the more firmly new information is "woven in neurologically." There is greater depth of meaning when new information is connected to existing knowledge. The lesson opening, therefore, should be structured to help students recall what they already know, understand the relevance of what they will learn, and be aware of what they will know and be able to do as a result of the learning activity. In other words, students should consciously connect new learning to previous learning. The teacher facilitates this process through effective opening activities.

Teaching Strategies/Activities (Input)

Teaching strategies are selected based on the type of content to be taught and the needs and abilities of the students. *Teaching strategies* are what the teacher does to develop background and set the stage for the learning activities students will engage in. Strategies may include demonstrating, modeling, explaining, and questioning. The input provided at this point gives students enough information to proceed confidently with the learning tasks. It does not preclude exploration and discovery on their part.

Student Activities

To learn, a student engages in some activity. The teacher selects or develops an instructional activity that "fits" the learning standard and the students' needs and abilities. An instructional activity is always related to the learning standard—it is not an end in itself. A learning activity may be as simple as reading a text passage, or it may be a more complex activity such as gathering data from multiple sources for problem solving. Today, an abundance of instructional activities is offered in teaching manuals, professional journals, books, newsletters, software, and on the Internet. Far more activities are available than can possibly be used by any given teacher or student. The teacher must be selective.

Effective learning activities enable students to reach specified standards. Several aspects of learning must be considered as learning activities are developed. This is not as simple as it may sound. Whether or not students are interested in an activity has an impact on their motivation to complete the activity, which affects their attention to the task and how much learning they will retain (Cummings, 1980). Therefore learning activities should be appealing and interesting to students. Activities should also be at an appropriate level of challenge to maintain interest—neither too easy nor too difficult. Knowing the range of students' abilities helps in planning activities that have an appropriate level of challenge. Activities should also be efficient, not overly complicated, and take only the amount of time necessary for learning to occur.

Types of Student Learning Activities. Student learning may be categorized according to the type of thinking it involves. Some learning is *literal;* it involves understanding and remembering information, facts, or steps in a process. It includes relatively simple activities for acquiring basic information and facts.

In *relational learning,* students connect or unite information or concepts from one or more sources including their own background knowledge and prior understandings. The thinking process involves associations between new learning and previously learned material.

Transformational learning involves students in transcribing and applying what they know in a different way. Transformational thinking becomes more complex and involves converting new learning through known applications.

Extensional learning activities ask students to take their learning and extend it using literal, relational, and transformational strategies to create, produce, originate, evaluate, and in other ways exhibit their learning in a unique way. Examples of types of learning activities are shown in Figure 1.6.

The categorization of learning into literal, relational, transformational, and extensional domains allows teachers to use the wording of state learning standards as they plan lessons. The categories are not totally isolated, separate entities; there is a degree of overlap. Strictly defined, separate categories of learning activities are probably not possible, but understanding general categories of learning helps to focus the planning of activities in relation to the learning standards. An important caveat to this categorization of learning activities is that all students should participate in all types of learning. It would be a drastic mistake to treat these categories as a hierarchy in which students begin with literal learning, staying there until the teacher decides mastery is obtained and then moving on to the next category. Linear use of learning categories is neither indicated nor effective. It is contrary to theory and research, which suggests an overlap and integration of the various types of thinking (Good & Brophy, 1997). It is not possible to totally isolate levels of thinking into separate compartments; they are interrelated and iterative (Ellis & Fouts, 1997).

Describing Learning Activities. The wording of the learning standard is a guide to the teacher in developing learning activities. The wording of the learning activity guides the students in the learning task. Therefore, a critical part of instructional planning is the description, explanation, or directions for a learning activity. The wording of the description is carefully chosen to convey

---

Types of Learning Activities

Literal Learning. Literal learning includes relatively simple activities for acquiring basic information and facts. The following are examples of literal learning activities:

- State the steps in the scientific method.
- Tell the name of the president of the United States during the Great Depression.
- Match the generals to their Civil War battles.

Relational Learning. In relational learning, students relate or connect information from one or more sources including their own background knowledge. Some examples of relational learning activities are as follows:

- Locate the ancient civilization of Mesopotamia on a modern-day map.
- Compare the populations of Illinois and Chicago over the last century.
- Predict the next action in a story.

Transformational Learning. Transformational learning requires the student to transcribe or apply learning in a different way. Some examples of transformational learning activities are as follows:

- Rewrite the ending to a story.
- Demonstrate the operation of a simple machine.
- Dramatize a historical event.

Extensional Learning. Extensional learning activities ask students to take their learning and extend it using literal, relational, and transformational strategies to create, produce, originate, evaluate, and in other ways exhibit their learning in a unique way. Some examples are as follows:

- Critique a novel.
- Design a rubric for a learning task and use it to assess the task.
- Justify the actions of the main character in a story.

Figure 1.6   Types of Learning Activities

precisely what students are to accomplish. Selecting appropriate terminology for the learning activity is necessary to design coherent and organized instruction. If the students are asked only to *list* events in chronological order, it is not fair to expect that they will *analyze* those events. If *analysis* behavior is expected, the terminology that conveys this expectation must be used. The key word in the description of an instructional activity is the linchpin and, therefore, must be carefully chosen. The key word is a verb that indicates the action of the student in the learning process. For example: "*Compare* the educational systems of the United States and Canada." A list of suggested terms (verbs) for learning activities is contained in Figure 1.7. Teachers may find it helpful to refer to this list in describing instructional activities.

Engaged Learning. How students learn is just as important as what they learn. Student engagement is a high-priority consideration in instructional design. Danielson (1996, p. 95) states, "Engaging students in learning is the raison d'être of education. All other components are in the service of student engagement." But engaged learning activities are not selected merely for their hands-on quality and potential for enjoyment. The purpose of engagement is to heighten students' interest and motivation as they learn important concepts,

Student engagement is a high-priority consideration in instructional design.

Designing Learning Activities: Terms to Use

Use the following terms to design instructional activities that correspond to the learning standard.

Literal Learning

Count	Identify	Outline
Define	Label	Quote
Find	List	Recall
	Match	Tell
	Name	

Relational Learning

Compare	Discuss	Predict
Conclude	Explain	Report
Contrast	Generalize	Restate
Demonstrate	Interpret	Review
Describe	Locate	Sequence
Differentiate	Measure	Show
	Paraphrase	Summarize

Transformational Learning

Analyze	Debate	Research
Apply	Deduce	Rewrite
Change	Demonstrate	Select
Characterize	Diagram	Separate
Choose	Distinguish	Use
Collect	Dramatize	
Compute	Examine	

Extensional Learning

Appraise	Criticize	Judge	Prioritize
Assess	Decide	Justify	Produce
Choose	Design	Make up	Propose
Compose	Develop	Originate	Prove
Conclude	Evaluate	Perform	Rank
Construct	Integrate	Plan	Rate
Create	Invent	Pretend	

Figure 1.7   Designing Learning Activities: Terms to Use

skills, and processes. Students are engaged when they are involved in planning, setting goals for their learning, choosing activities, and even developing assessments. Engagement provides the conditions in which concepts are made meaningful.

Brain-Compatible Activities. Recent research into how the brain learns provides a rich source of information for teachers as they plan instruction. Humans organize ideas, concepts, beliefs, attitudes, opinions, and emotions in complex mental networks called "schema." *Schemata* are the building blocks of cognition (Rumelhart, 1982). When new ideas and concepts are connected to existing schemata, they become part of it (Sousa, 2005). Effective teaching therefore helps students connect new concepts to their existing prior knowledge. Students must activate the appropriate schema that fits the particular learning context (Vacca, 2002). Blachowicz and Ogle (2001) explain the importance of connecting one's prior knowledge during reading as an ongoing process that not only facilitates comprehension but is necessary for it.

Humans organize ideas, concepts, beliefs, attitudes, opinions, and emotions in complex mental networks call "schema."

Teachers frame instruction around brain-compatible learning to maximize learning. Robin Fogarty (1997) tells us that brain-compatible classrooms differ from others in three major ways. First, brain-compatible learning is integrated, not isolated. Second, threat and anxiety are diminished, allowing students to function at high levels. And third, learning involves real or simulated "whole" experiences that tap into many ways of thinking, expressing, and doing.

Teachers use many effective brain-based strategies to deepen students' understanding. The engaged learning activities in Figure 1.8 are adapted from the work of Eric Jensen (2000). These activities involve students and provide opportunities for them to do something with information and concepts they are learning. The common elements of all these activities are applying, transforming, and extending concepts and information through communicating and creating. These activities engage students in learning by allowing them to *do* something, to *use* concepts, ideas, strategies, and processes. This use and manipulation of material is the vehicle to deepen understanding by weaving it into existing knowledge.

Closing/Summary/Reflection

When one connects new learning to prior knowledge, one's mental map of information, concepts, skills, processes, attitudes, values, and beliefs related to a topic is expanded. This mental map is the schema or linked collection of related thoughts and ideas and is the operating base within which new information is integrated. The schema is expanded and understanding deepened through metacognitive processing and reflection. Seifert (1999) states that reflection is the partner of experience. Reflection and experience lead us to construct meaning. It is therefore important that students have opportunities for metacognitive processing throughout, and especially at the conclusion of, a learning experience. Notebook journals, audio journals, and sketch pads are some means for students to reflect and record the impact of their learning and thinking.

Engaged Learning Activities

1. Graphic Organizers

Use graphic organizers to create mind maps for students, thereby strengthening learning and subsequent recall of material. When the graphic organizers are personalized to match the needs and backgrounds of the students, they become even more powerful. A slightly different twist is to use pictures or drawings instead of words to create a mind map.

2. Creative Retelling

Weave content information into a story using known genres such as fables, tall tales, songs, and myths. In this manner, the information is transformed into a different setting.

3. Peer Presenting

Use an "each one, teach one" model, or in some manner allow students to teach each other. Explaining strengthens understanding.

4. Model Making

Create models (two- or three-dimensional) to produce a concrete representation of an abstract concept.

5. Performance

Transform information or a concept into a performance using drama, music, or dance. Write about the solution to a math problem or create a poem about a science concept.

6. Role Playing

Provide simulated experiences by having some students assume the role of historical or fictional characters while other students take on the role of reporter in an interview activity.

7. Debate, Discuss, Debrief

Provide opportunities for students to explain their thinking in a nonthreatening environment. Communication is the key for deepening understanding.

8. Game Making

Use a known game genre into which the new concepts and material are incorporated.

9. Presentations

Provide opportunities for students to use technology or visual aids or to process information and transform it for others.

SOURCE: Jensen, E. (2000). *Brain-Based Learning*. San Diego, CA: The Brain Store.

Figure 1.8   Engaged Learning Activities

Materials/Resources

The variety of instructional materials available is extensive and at times overwhelming. Learning resources and materials must, of course, be appropriate to the needs and interests of the students. Sometimes the only materials needed are a pencil and paper (or word processor). Other times, more extensive resources are needed for exploration and research. Generally the teacher selects learning resources for young learners. But as students take more responsibility for their learning, they begin to search out information and learning resources on their own. Guidance and support at this stage helps students become independent learners and users of the vast number of resources at their disposal.

Although the practice is not as prevalent today as in the past, some schools use a commercial textbook program as the required curriculum. When this is the case, state or district learning standards are used as a filter in selecting what is important to teach from the textbook. A comparison of learning standards and textbook objectives points out instructional priorities and enables the teacher to eliminate some textbook material. This standards-driven approach makes the curriculum more manageable.

Technology-related materials can support and enhance student learning. However, as with all materials, those that are technology based should be carefully chosen. Technology to support teaching the learning standards is the foremost consideration. Some technology-based applications can include the following:

- Explore a concept using videos, computer software programs, or Web sites.

- Present a concept or idea using videos or presentation software such as PowerPoint.

- Analyze and sort data and information using database programs.

- Create artistic products using graphic and sound design.

Other resources for learning extend beyond the classroom into the community. Partnerships with governmental agencies, local businesses, and professional organizations can be a source of extended learning opportunities for students. Joining resources helps build greater understanding of the relationship between schooling and real-world applications.

Practice and Follow-up Activities

Not all students progress at the same pace. Monitoring and observing students during the lesson will indicate which students need more instruction or practice. For these students, it is appropriate to provide additional activities to reinforce learning. Practice activities should be interesting, well designed, and assigned only as necessary. Teachers find it helpful to keep a file of related worksheets and activities for these occasions.

Assessment

Assessment of student learning typically occurs at the conclusion of the lesson. The assessment provides feedback to the student and the teacher and gives direction for future lesson planning.

Performance Expectations

Performance expectations describe how well students are expected to do on the assessment. Expectations are often in the form of a grading scale. The decision as to cutoff points for grades or "passing" is made before the assessment is given and is made known to all students.

Timing the Lesson

The amount of time necessary for a lesson is an important planning consideration. The teacher must allocate a reasonable amount of time for students to learn new concepts and balance this with the amount of total time in the school year (or semester) available to teach the required curriculum. It may be enjoyable to spend three weeks on a dinosaur unit, but in terms of how much time is required for the entire curriculum, it may not be reasonable. It is important to know the curriculum and determine how much time is to be allocated to each segment.

The amount of time available in a class period is also considered as the lesson is developed. The school calendar and the daily schedule will impact how much time is available for each lesson. The nature of the lesson itself is another consideration in determining the amount of time allotted. Concepts that involve analysis or synthesis may require a longer time period or extend over several class periods. Less complex learning that involves presentation of factual information may not require as much time.

It is important to allocate a reasonable amount of time for a lesson, but it is equally important to maintain flexibility. If a lesson ends with 10 minutes to spare, it is good practice to have a follow-up activity in place that can be tapped into. Likewise, if a lesson requires more than the allotted time, adjustments in the daily or weekly schedule will be required. A summary of the lesson plan components is shown in Figure 1.9.

USING THE BASIC INSTRUCTIONAL DESIGN PLANNING GUIDE

An effective basic lesson is developed when the teacher understands the components of the lesson planning process and carefully thinks through each of the components: standards and performance descriptors, assessment, and the lesson itself, which includes teaching strategies and student activities. The Basic Instructional Design Planning Guide (Figure 1.10) is a tool to assist teachers in thinking through all the components of an effective lesson. It comprises three sections: Section 1: Desired Results—Standards and Performance Descriptors; Section 2: Assessment—Evidence of Learning; and Section 3: Lesson Design. Each of these three sections includes three columns: "Planning Questions and Decisions," "Information and Data Sources," and "Notes and Comments." The Planning Questions and Decisions column poses a series of key questions to guide and stimulate thinking during the planning process. The Information and Data Sources column lists the types of resources and data sources that will facilitate answering the questions in column one. The Notes and Comments column provides information that will further clarify and assist in answering questions in column one.

Summary of Components of an Effective Lesson Plan

- Statement of what is to be taught (standards/performance descriptors)

- Introduction or opening of the lesson
  The introduction sets the stage and motivates students to engage in the lesson activity.

- Teaching strategies
  The teacher models, explains, demonstrates, or otherwise presents what students are to learn.

- Student activities
  Students engage in learning new concepts or reinforcing what the teacher has presented.

- Closing/summary/reflection
  The conclusion of the lesson provides opportunities for students to reflect on their learning and/or summarize what they have accomplished.

- Materials/resources
  Materials are available that assist students in practicing the concepts presented in the lesson.

- Practice and follow-up assignments
  Additional activities are assigned as needed.

- Assessment
  Students are assessed in relation to the learning standard.

- Performance expectations
  Expectations for performance on the assessment are clearly defined and communicated.

- Timing
  Sufficient time is allocated to the learning activity.

Figure 1.9   Summary of Components of an Effective Lesson Plan

Below are suggestions for using the planning guide:

1. Read the planning guide in its entirety.

It is good practice to become thoroughly familiar with the planning guide before using it. Doing so saves time in the long run. Get the "big picture" in mind before filling in the details.

2. Think it through.

Begin with Section 1: Desired Results—Standards and Performance Descriptors. Think about the questions in column one of the planning guide and write down your thoughts and ideas. Consult the data and information sources suggested in column two. Think about your current teaching assignment and the data and information you have available as well as what you may need to obtain. The Notes and Comments column provides further information to consider. Continue through Section 2: Assessment—Evidence of Learning and Section 3: Lesson Design. The result of your thinking provides the foundation for a well-designed, effective lesson. An example of the thinking process of a middle school science teacher is shown in Figure 1.11. A Basic Instructional Design Preliminary Planning reproducible (pp. 31–32) is provided to record your thinking.

   3.   Synthesize the information.

   The thinking process described above provides a great deal of information which now must be synthesized into a coherent plan for instruction. The lesson plan specifies the instructional process that will occur in the classroom. An example of a lesson plan for a Grade 7 science class is shown in Figure 1.12. An example of a lesson plan for Grade 1 reading is shown in Figure 1.13. A reproducible master is included for lesson planning.

   Preservice and novice teachers will find it helpful to follow all the steps in the guide. When teachers become very familiar with the planning guide, they are able to take shortcuts in planning by using the lesson plan form without filling out the planning guide. This shortcut is possible when the planning questions are practiced and well known. Understanding the thinking process involved in planning a basic lesson makes subsequent planning easier and provides a foundation for planning more complex instruction.

REFLECTIVE PRACTICE: INNER DIALOGUE

Merely following an outline or filling in a template is not sufficient to develop skill in instructional design. Planning is a metacognitive, reflective process in which the teacher thinks, reflects, adjusts, and fine-tunes the various components until a coherent plan emerges. When reflection is an intrinsic part of the instructional design process and teachers take time to analyze their planning efforts, they learn through their experiences, and future planning becomes more effective and efficient.

   What Costa (1991) called "inner dialogue" is essential to professional growth, change, and improvement. Reflection is important to the planning process. Planning is a skill, and it becomes stronger with experience and practice. As with all learning, reflection deepens understanding. The Inner Dialogue page in Figure 1.14 is provided for reflections on the planning process, including pros and cons, benefits, and challenges.

BASIC INSTRUCTIONAL DESIGN PLANNING GUIDE

SECTION 1: Desired Results—Standards and Performance Descriptors	

Lessons are grounded on standards and performance descriptors. Use these questions to plan a basic lesson.

Planning Questions and Decisions	Information and Data Sources	Notes and Comments
1. What do students need to learn? What is the specific learning standard/performance descriptor to be taught?	District curriculum guides, district and state standards documents Student needs as determined by test data (formal and informal), school improvement goals, district goals	What students need to learn is the first critical question a teacher considers in planning. A decision regarding what is to be taught is made before selecting or designing learning activities. A clear statement of what students are to do provides clarity and focus in planning.

Figure 1.10   Basic Instructional Design Planning Guide

SECTION 2: Assessment—Evidence of Learning

Assessment of students must be aligned to what students should know and be able to do as defined in the learning standards and performance descriptors. Use these questions as a thinking guide to plan assessment procedures.

Planning Questions and Decisions	Information and Data Sources	Notes and Comments
1. How will students demonstrate what they have learned?	See curriculum resource information and best practices information related to types of assessment: criterion-referenced assessment, standardized assessment, performance assessment, and in-class observation.	Assessments must be valid and reliable indicators of students' performance.
2. What assessment materials are available and what materials need to be developed?	Assessment items are often part of textbook materials. District or school assessments may be available and in some cases required.	Select an assessment strategy that is aligned to what is being taught. Commercially prepared assessments have often been field tested for reliability. Be sure the test relates directly to the learning standard and performance descriptor. Teacher-made tests can be tricky to develop. Whenever possible, try out a teacher-made assessment (perhaps with another class) before using it to evaluate students.
3. How will the assessment be evaluated or scored?	Scoring keys are efficient for limited-response items. Electronic scoring may be more efficient if appropriate. Rubrics for written responses may be available in district curriculum guides, teacher manuals, and other sources.	Consistency is important in assessment. Students should be assessed in a like manner unless there is a valid, documented reason for not doing so.
4. How will assessment results be reported?	Grading scales, report cards, or portfolios may be required. If feasible, electronic data may also be useful.	In addition to assessment, consider instructional feedback to students based on assessment results.
5. What further practice and follow-up assessment can be provided for students who fall below expectations?	Additional commercially developed or teacher-prepared activities may be used for further practice. Alternative test forms may be used for retesting.	It is efficient to have a file of alternative practice activities and test forms available when needed. Consider creating or selecting these as the lesson is developed.
6. How will the assessment results be used?	Be aware of district policies and handbooks that describe the use of assessment results.	Use assessment results to determine student strengths and weaknesses and plan the next lessons.

Figure 1.10 (Continued)

SECTION 3: Lesson Design

Learning activities and teaching strategies are based on what students need to learn and how they will be assessed. Use these questions as a thinking guide to plan a basic lesson.

Planning Questions and Decisions	Information and Data Sources	Notes and Comments
1. What is the specific learning standard or performance descriptor addressed in the lesson?	See Section 1 of this planning guide.	Maintain focus on the specific standard and performance descriptor in developing all aspects of the lesson plan.
2. What is a motivating opening for the lesson?	Curriculum guides, teaching manuals, professional literature, best practices information, etc., are sources of information for lesson development.	
3. What teaching strategies will be effective?		Consider use of electronic resources and other technological materials.
4. What learning activities will students engage in?		
5. What opportunities will students have to reflect on their learning?		
6. What materials and resources are needed to support and enhance learning?		Use the Lesson Plan template to consolidate, summarize, and sequence the lesson information.
7. How will student progress be monitored?		
8. What forms of follow-up practice may be used?		
9. How long will the lesson take?		
10. Are there any foreseeable pitfalls in this lesson?		
11. What alternatives are there if the lesson doesn't work out?		

Figure 1.10 (Continued)

BASIC INSTRUCTIONAL DESIGN PLANNING GUIDE: EXAMPLE FROM GRADE 7 SCIENCE

SECTION 1: Desired Results—Standards and Performance Descriptors

Lessons are grounded on standards and performance descriptors. Use these questions to plan a basic lesson.

1. **What do students need to learn? What is the specific learning standard/performance descriptor to be taught?**

   Students will distinguish between mixtures that are solutions and those that are not.

   This performance descriptor is part of the district curriculum in understanding solutions. It aligns to the state and the National Science Teachers Association (NSTA) standards.

Figure 1.11   Basic Instructional Design Planning Guide: Example From Grade 7 Science

SECTION 2: Assessment—Evidence of Learning

1. How will students demonstrate their learning?	Science log entry of experiment—steps and conclusions	Selected-response test (20 items including multiple choice and short answer)	Present oral report of experiment and conclusions to class. This is an ongoing activity. A few students will do an oral presentation for each major unit of study.
2. What assessment materials are available and what materials need to be developed?	Use standard format provided by the Science Department.	Textbook	Develop description of the oral presentation to go along with the rubric.
3. How will the assessment be scored?	Rubric provided by the Science Department	Answer key (20 items, 5 points each) Use Scantron for scoring.	Generic presentation rubric
4. How will the assessment be reported?	Copy of rubric showing performance level will be returned to students. Teacher comments will be included as appropriate. Provide time for student conferences if requested by student or for students who need additional personal feedback.	Grades will be determined according to the schoolwide grading scale. Go over test items with students.	Copy of rubric showing performance level will be returned to students. Teacher comments will be included as appropriate.
5. What further practice and follow-up assessment can be provided for students who fall below expectations?	Return science log to student with feedback on what is needed to meet expectations. Students make revisions as necessary (before scheduling oral presentation).	Select alternative activities in teacher's manual for reinforcement of content. (Unit 3, pages 101–109)	A follow-up assessment is not available.
6. How will the assessment results be used?	Determine which students need additional practice. Include results in quarterly report card grade.	Determine which students need reinforcement of content information. Students make corrections as necessary—no extra credit. Include results in quarterly report card grade.	The rubric will provide feedback to the student. A total of 20 points will be included in the student's final report card grade.

Figure 1.11 (Continued)

SECTION 3: Lesson Design

1. What is the specific learning standard or performance descriptor addressed in the lesson?
Students will distinguish between mixtures that are solutions and those that are not.

2. What is a motivating opening for the lesson?
Set up as a problem-solving activity related to a real-life application: forensic scientist working with a detective to solve a criminal case. Show two containers of liquid and ask how they would identify the one that has water and the one that contains another substance. Ask students why such identification is necessary or important. Record responses for later review.

3. What teaching strategies will be effective?
Possibilities include the following: Review and develop background information through discussion, reading, research, and questioning the teacher. Use KWL strategy. Invite a chemist from local industry to talk with students about real-life applications. Conduct demonstration or experiment. Use lab record/report activity.

4. In what learning activities will students engage?
Students will conduct a lab experiment in groups of three.
Students will record the experiment procedure and outcomes in their personal lab books.
Whole-class discussion of findings and outcomes.

5. What materials are needed for this lesson?
Safety goggles, lab aprons, graduated cylinders, clear plastic glasses or beakers, stirring rods, six prepared mixtures (water/milk, water/sugar, water/oil, water/rubbing alcohol, water/drink mix, sand/salt).
For Tyndall effect: Flashlight, cardboard, metric ruler, pencil.
Also, students may keep notes on word-processing program. The computer probe equipment is also a possibility—perhaps as a demonstration.

6. What opportunities will students have to reflect on their learning?
At the conclusion of the lesson, students will write on three new things they learned as a result of the lesson and how these three things have application to their everyday life. (This could be part of the assessment.)

7. How will student progress be monitored?
During lab work, the teacher will observe students and check for proper use of equipment and following directions. Spot checks of lab book entries will be made.

8. What forms of additional practice may be necessary?
Students who miss this session or need further input may review textbook diagrams and explanations of the Tyndall effect and solutions. A video disc segment on solutions may be viewed. Or, they could partner with another student to review science log entries.

9. How long will the lesson take?
Two class periods will be scheduled for this lesson. I may have to provide additional time to get all presentations in—or I could have just a few groups present. Other groups could present for other lessons.

10. Are there any foreseeable pitfalls in this lesson?
Students must perform the experiment carefully to obtain the desired results. Students will need teacher supervision and direction in carrying out the experiment to ensure safety and proper use of lab equipment. Extra mixtures will be available in case of spills.

11. What alternatives are there if the lesson doesn't work out?
A demonstration will be used if the student activity doesn't work out as planned. Students will observe and record their findings in their science logs.

Figure 1.11 (Continued)

Lesson Plan—Grade 7 Science

Learning Standard (concepts, skills, processes)

Students will differentiate between mixtures that are solutions and those that are not.

Lesson Design	Materials	Student Grouping Arrangement
• **Opening (outcomes/purpose/expectations)** Describe problem scenario: A forensic scientist is working with a detective to solve a criminal case. Show two beakers. Ask: How can the scientist tell which beaker contains water and which contains a mixture of salt and water? Discuss responses. Record responses for later review. Ask: Why is it important to be able to identify substances?	Beakers/mixtures Chart paper, markers	Whole class
• **Teaching Strategies/Activities (demonstration, modeling, explanation, directions, etc.)** Describe lab setup and activity. (Refer to lab activity manual) Review lab safety. Distribute/review experiment procedure.		
• **Student Activities** Complete lab activity. Record findings in lab manual.	Safety glasses, lab aprons, graduated cylinders, clear beakers, stirring rods, six prepared mixtures, testing substances as listed in activity manual	Three students per group (prearranged by teacher) Lab manual entries—individual
• **Closing (connections/summary/reflection)** Groups 1, 2, and 3 to report findings. Compare results. Verbalize conclusions. Review opening activity discussion. Discuss what was learned in the lab activity. Record two or more important concepts from this experiment in lab manual.		Whole class Lab manual entry—individual
Practice Activities/Assignments View video disc segment on this experiment and record results in lab manual.		Individual or small group, depending on who is absent. Arrange with resource center for viewing and completion of work.
Assessment of Student Learning 1. In small groups, students will use the rubric to evaluate their lab manual entries. 2. 20-item completion test on content.		

Figure 1.12   Lesson Plan—Grade 7 Science

Lesson Plan—Grade 1 Reading

Learning Standard(s) (concepts, skills, processes)

1. Guided reading nonfiction: "What Ants Can Do"
2. Review short /a/ sound

Assessment of Learning Standard

1. Observation of students during oral reading
2. Picture essay of what ants can do
3. Transfer short /a/ sound to identifying other words

Lesson Design	Materials	Student Grouping
• **Opening (outcomes/purpose/expectations)** 1. Discussion—Poster of ant colony (build background) 2. Recognize short /a/ sound from words read aloud 3. Write a-n-t	Poster Chart paper Markers List of short /a/ words	Guided reading Group 1: Leslie, Mary, Dennis, Larry, Joni

• **Teaching Strategies/Activities (demonstration, modeling, explanation, directions, etc.)**
 	
1. Model letter/sound segmentation
2. Guided reading of text
  • Discussion of details in pictures
  • Compare ants to other insects
  • Generate specific questions about ants throughout reading
3. Explain and reinforce short /a/ sound
	Guided reading books: *Ants* by Judy Nayer	

• **Student Activities** 1. Silent and oral reading 2. Picture essay 3. Write *a-n-t* 4. List other words with short /a/ sound	Booklets Crayons Pencils	
• **Closing (connections/summary/reflection)** 1. Discuss picture essays 2. Ask: What did you learn about ants? 3. Ask: What do ants remind you of? (Connect to other types of insects.)	Other insect books.	
Practice Activities/Assignments 1. Worksheet on short /a/ sound 2. Self-selected reading on ants and other insects from classroom library sets	Worksheet on short /a/ sound	
Assessment 1. Watch for application of short /a/ sound 2. Evaluate worksheet on short /a/ sound	Student checklist to observe and record use of short /a/	

Figure 1.13   Lesson Plan—Grade 1 Reading

Inner Dialogue

Reflect on the planning process to deepen your understanding. Keep your notes and refer to them when you plan again.

This is what I did in the planning process.	This is what I think about it and how I might change or modify it.
Some new learning	
Some benefits	
Some challenges	

Figure 1.14   Inner Dialogue

BASIC INSTRUCTIONAL DESIGN
PRELIMINARY PLANNING

Desired Results	1. What learning standards will be taught?
Evidence of Learning	2. How will students demonstrate what they have learned?
	3. What assessment materials are available and what materials need to be developed?
	4. How will the assessment be scored or evaluated?
	5. How will assessment results be reported?
	6. What practice and follow-up assessment can be provided for students who fall below expectations?
	7. How will assessment results be used?

(Continued)

(Continued)

Lesson Design	8. What is a motivating opening for the lesson?
	9. What teaching strategies will be effective?
	10. What learning activities will students engage in?
	11. What opportunities will students have to reflect on their learning?
	12. What materials and resources are needed to support and enhance learning?
	13. How will student progress be monitored?
	14. What forms of follow-up practice may be used?
	15. How long will the lesson take?
	16. Are there any foreseeable pitfalls in the lesson?
	17. What alternatives are there if the lesson does not work out?

BASIC LESSON PLAN

Learning Standards (concepts, skills, processes)

Lesson Design	Materials	Student Grouping
• **Opening** (outcomes/purpose/expectations)		
• **Teaching Strategies/Activities** (demonstration, modeling, explanation, directions, etc.)		
• **Student Activities**		
• **Closing** (connections/summary/reflection)		
Practice Activities/Assignments		
Assessment of Student Learning		

Date: **Time:**

Notes/Comments:

Integrated Instructional Design

2

Integrated instruction, sometimes referred to as thematic or interdisciplinary instruction, most likely has its roots in the progressive education movement of the early 1900s (Drake, 1993; Rippa, 1988). John Dewey emphasized the advantages of engaging students in real-world experiences and criticized instructional methods that focused learning into separate, isolated compartments. His belief in the importance of experience as a method of teaching is shown in the following statement:

> Our whole policy of compulsory education rises or falls with our ability to make school life an interesting and absorbing experience to the child. In one sense, there is no such thing as compulsory education. We can have compulsory physical attendance at school; but education comes only through willing attention to and participation in school activities. It follows that the teacher must select these activities with reference to the child's interests, powers, and capacities. In no other way can she guarantee that the child will be present. (Dewey, 1913, p. ix)

AN INTEGRATED APPROACH TO LEARNING

Integrated instruction combines learning standards from two or more content areas within a single lesson or unit of study. The learning standards are connected through activities and tasks in a logical manner so that students are able to understand relationships among the standards. Assessment of student progress is likewise connected and embedded in the activities. Assessment of several learning standards may be covered in one test.

Genuine learning occurs as students see the connections among concepts and weave these concepts into their own scheme of meaning.

An integrated approach to learning provides continuity and order for students. It helps them make sense of and see associations among the seeming randomness of educational objectives (Zemelman, Daniels, & Hyde, 1993). Genuine learning occurs as students see the connections among concepts and weave these connections into their own scheme of meaning (Beane, 1993). An integrated curriculum helps students connect specific learning standards as they construct knowledge. Integrated instructional designs range from the

35

combination of a few learning standards to total curriculum integration based on a major theme.

WHY INTEGRATED INSTRUCTION IS A GOOD IDEA

Understanding relationships and connections is far more valuable than knowing isolated bits and pieces of information (Withrow, Long, & Marx, 1999). The brain searches for patterns and connections within experiences to make sense of the world (Caine & Caine, 1991). Experiences that provide opportunities for students to make connections are likely to provide more lasting and deeper learning. The propensity of the human brain to search for patterns of meaning is the reasoning behind integrated instruction (Jensen, 2000). Shanahan (1997) reports that student motivation in integrated learning settings is greater than in traditional settings, and integrated instruction produces positive attitudes toward learning. While few empirical studies have been done to test the effectiveness of integrated learning (Gavelek, Raphael, Biondo, & Wang, 2000), proponents of this approach base their support on the positive experiences and observations of classrooms where integrated learning flourishes (Guthrie & McCann, 1997).

Experiences that provide opportunities for students to make connecitons are likely to provide more lasting and deeper meaning.

The theoretical basis for integrated instruction is also found in constructivist theory, which explains that learning occurs as a person builds meaning through direct experience (Ellis & Fouts, 1997). Learning is less fragmented when standards are meaningfully integrated into a unit of instruction. Science, social studies, physical development, fine arts, and language arts standards that are related and combined in learning experiences provide students with logical connections among the content areas. It makes sense for students to hone their skills in reading and writing by applying them in the science, social studies, health, and fine arts curricula. Doing so creates a valid purpose for using reading and writing.

BENEFITING FROM BEST PRACTICE MODELS

The predominant factors that seem to deter teachers from using an integrated instructional approach are lack of time for planning and instruction, access to professional development, and availability of practical models. Even when teachers are convinced of the effectiveness of integrated instruction and motivated to use it, the lack of practical models may discourage them (Gehrke, 1993).

Teachers need time to plan, especially with one another, to integrate standards across content areas. Otherwise the task may be too monumental for any one teacher to assume (Jacobs, 1991a). Just as students benefit from working in teams, so do teachers when there is a feeling of shared responsibility.

In spite of the advantages associated with integrated instruction, American education today, for the most part, remains structured around separate disciplines or content areas (Beane, 1993; Ellis & Fouts, 1997; Jacobs, 1991a).

At the high school level, the student's day is an assortment of seven or eight unrelated, disjointed time periods (Zemelman et al., 1993). And, in the classroom, where the curriculum is translated into instruction, instruction is most likely to be a series of isolated lessons. Some high schools have shown progress toward integrated learning by combining English, literature, history, and civics in an American Studies course. Most often, this type of course is team taught by content area certified teachers.

Students need time to actively engage in learning, process their learning, and reflect on their learning (Caine & Caine, 1991; Fogarty, 1996). The traditional 45-minute time period schedule predominant in today's high schools does not lend itself to the type of teaching that promotes integrated, connected learning. Many teachers report that with a 45-minute period, there is little they can do other than the traditional lecture, question-respond strategy. Some middle schools and high schools have changed from the shorter periods to longer blocks of time to promote more connected learning through integrated instruction (Canady & Rettig, 1995). Longer blocks of time enable teachers to actively involve students in learning.

If teachers are to change the way they teach, they need ongoing professional development (Withrow et al., 1999). Effective professional development not only points out best practices but also provides practical, realistic models—a structure for learning, transferring, and applying new approaches (Moye, 1997). Professional development related to integrated instruction prepares teachers with strategies for successful implementation.

WHAT GETS INTEGRATED?

Some learning standards have a natural connection, some are mutually reinforcing, and some can be threaded through a "big idea" or theme. Examples of types of standard connections are described below.

Some learning standards have a natural connection. For example, combining graphing with reporting scientific data not only makes sense in terms of saving instructional time; it is also more meaningful for students. They use graphing for a real purpose.

Some learning standards are mutually reinforcing. For example, when students write about something they have read (short story) or done (science experiment), they communicate their comprehension and understanding and reinforce their writing skills.

Some learning standards are threaded through a big idea. For example, the study of people in societies combines learning standards from history, geography, government and civics, economics, anthropology, and sociology (Lewis, 1993). The focus or emphasis during such a unit of study may shift from history to economics to sociology depending on the learning standards being addressed.

Curriculum integration may be approached in a variety of ways. Robin Fogarty (1991) presents 10 models of curriculum integration approaches. She begins by explaining the traditional, separate disciplines model and then describes the integrated models as summarized in Figure 2.1.

Fogarty's Models of Curriculum Integration

Fragmented—The traditional model of separate and distinct disciplines, which fragments the subject areas.

Connected—Within each subject area, course content is connected topic to topic, concept to concept, one year's work to the next, and relates ideas(s) explicitly.

Nested—Within each subject area, the teacher targets multiple skills: a social skill, a thinking skill, and a content-specific skill.

Sequenced—Topics or units of study are rearranged and sequenced to coincide with one another. Similar ideas are taught in concert while remaining separate subjects.

Shared—Shared planning and teaching take place in two disciplines in which overlapping concepts or ideas emerge as organizing elements.

Webbed—A major theme is selected and the learning concepts of all the disciplines are examined to determine a "fit" with the major theme. Once the learning concepts are outlined, instructional activities are designed around them. (This is probably the most popular approach to integrating the curriculum.)

Threaded—The metacurricular approach threads thinking skills, social skills, multiple intelligences, technology, and study skills through the various disciplines.

Integrated—This interdisciplinary approach matches subjects with overlaps in topics and concepts, using some team teaching in an authentic integrated model.

Immersed—The disciplines become part of the learner's lens of expertise; the learner filters all content through this lens and becomes immersed in his or her own experience.

Networked—The learner filters all learning through the expert's eye and makes internal connections that lead to external networks of experts in related fields.

SOURCE: Fogarty, Robin (1991), *How to Integrate the Curricula.* Thousand Oaks, CA: Corwin Press. Used with permission.

Figure 2.1   Fogarty's Model of Curriculum Integration

Any of the models described by Fogarty may be used to integrate the curriculum. A discussion among staff members on the pros and cons of these models helps to build common understandings and to develop a rationale for using a particular type of integrated instruction.

PLANNING INTEGRATED INSTRUCTION

An integrated lesson plan has the same components as the basic lesson plan; the major difference is that learning standards from two or more content areas are included. Moving from a basic lesson to an integrated lesson is a natural progression for many teachers as they become adept at lesson planning and see the big picture of the learning process.

Develop the Rationale for Integrated Instruction

A clearly defined rationale for using integrated instruction and an organized plan to facilitate smooth implementation must exist. As Relan and Kimpston (1993) point out, there should be clear reasons for selecting an integrated approach over some other. Brophy and Alleman (1991) likewise explain that teachers must be selective and astute in planning curriculum integration and beware of integration merely for the sake of integration. There should be a logical connection among the learning standards incorporated into the integrated plan and a clear, direct connection between the standards and the teaching and learning activities.

Make the Commitment

The first question to be addressed is why integrated instruction will best serve the students. A written statement affirming the value and use of integrated learning serves as a rationale, gives direction to the teaching staff, and communicates to parents and the community what students learn and how they will learn it.

Plan the Desired Results: Standards and Performance Descriptors

Standards and performance descriptors drive the planning process for integrated instruction. The learning standards that are already in place are the starting point for planning integrated instruction. The first task is to decide which learning standards will be taught in an integrated manner. This may be accomplished by examining the topics and associated learning standards covered in the curriculum and constructing a curriculum calendar map.

Construct the Curriculum Calendar Map

Once an affirmative decision to use integrated instruction is made, all teachers involved should participate in developing the curriculum calendar map. While it is possible for one teacher to design and implement integrated instruction for his or her classroom, the planning effort is more efficient when all teachers are involved. A schoolwide effort to integrate instruction includes all staff members in planning. A grade level effort includes all teachers of that grade level.

One of the first planning steps in designing integrated instruction is to construct a curriculum calendar map that lists the topics of study in various content areas and their sequence through the school year. Heidi Hayes Jacobs (1991b, 1997) describes a process of curriculum calendar mapping in which teachers plot out the topics that are being taught. Each teacher writes down the major topics of study for his or her content area for each month of the school year. The curriculum map shown in Figure 2.2 shows the order in which major topics are taught prior to the alignment process. It is a general overview showing what is taught and when it is taught. This map is an "inventory" of content covered at a particular grade level. Once the curriculum map is developed, content can be rearranged so topics are connected in some logical manner across the content areas. Social studies and language arts content may be aligned by following a common time sequence. The *Diary of Anne Frank* fits the time period World War II, while *Sarah Plain and Tall* fits the time period of the Westward Movement.

There should be a logical connection among the learning standards incorporated into the integrated plan and a clear, direct connection between the standards and the teaching and learning activities.

Curriculum Calendar Map for Grade 7 Team: Preliminary Listing Prior to Alignment

	Language Arts	Social Studies
September	Diary of Anne Frank	Westward Movement
October		
November	Sarah Plain and Tall	Civil War
December		
January	To Kill a Mockingbird	Industrial Revolution, World War I
February	Johnny Tremain	
March	"Paul Bunyan and the Winter of the Blue Snow"	Great Depression
April		World War II
May	"The Raven" and the "Coming of Daylight"	

Figure 2.2 Curriculum Calendar Map for Grade 7 Team: Preliminary Listing Prior to Alignment

When a team of seventh grade teachers analyzed the major topics shown on their curriculum map, they concluded that it would be fairly easy to rearrange the order in which novels are read by students. They also decided to remove some novels and add others that had a logical connection to the social studies content. They revised the "Curriculum Calendar Map" as shown in Figure 2.3. This seventh grade team also decided to use the same writing rubric for essays and informational writing in language arts and social studies classes. Students would use reading to learn and writing to express what is learned in both their language arts and social studies classes.

Likewise, mathematics and science standards often have a natural connection. Consider the following two performance descriptors:

Mathematics: The student will construct a line and bar graph for given data.

Science: The student will report scientific data in an appropriate manner.

Combining these performance descriptors into a lesson provides an opportunity for students to use graphing skills to report scientific data from an experiment they have conducted.

When a team of science and mathematics teachers examined their course content, they determined which concepts had a logical connection and could be taught together. They decided to develop a joint project in which students would apply mathematical concepts to scientific experiments. Rubrics for each project were developed to help students clearly understand the purpose and expectations for performance. This basic form of curriculum integration helps students connect and apply skills in more than one content area. This approach to designing integrated instruction begins with the current curriculum and adjusts the teaching sequence rather then starting from scratch.

Each of the topics on the curriculum calendar map is associated with specific learning standards. Once the topics are aligned, the next step is to examine the learning standards that are subsumed under each topic. Realigning the standards in this way and connecting them to mutually supportive learning activities is central to planning for integrated instruction. The alignment of standards makes it easier to plan integrated lessons and units of study.

The curriculum mapping procedure may bring to light needed or desired changes in content. The planning process requires teachers to be open-minded and flexible in making changes to the curriculum. The fact that a particular novel has always been taught at a particular time and grade level is not justification for having it remain so when another novel or reading activity may better reinforce and contribute to integrated learning.

Verify Content Through Learning Standards

Even when content is the initial starting point in developing an integrated lesson, content must be referenced to the learning standards. The content or topics must be translated and verified against the learning standards that are expected for a particular grade level. Content must reflect the learning standards. The Integrated Instruction Overview of Learning Standards (Figure 2.4 and the first reproducible) is used to document the learning standards within the content areas that

	Curriculum Calendar Map for Grade 7 Team: Listing of Major Topics After Alignment	
	Language Arts	**Social Studies**
September	Sarah Plain and Tall	Westward Movement
October		
November	To Kill a Mockingbird	Civil War
December		
January	Nothing but the Truth	Industrial Revolution, World War I
February		
March	Number the Stars	Great Depression
April	Diary of Anne Frank	World War II
May		

Figure 2.3 Curriculum Calendar Map for Grade 7 Team: Listing of Major Topics After Alignment

cluster around a major learning theme. This overview highlights and enables correction of redundancies and gaps in the curriculum. It may also be used to establish priorities and decide which standards are to be emphasized. Standards designated as having a high priority due to a weakness determined through student assessment data receive greater emphasis and focus during the lesson.

For integrated instruction to be effective, students must understand the patterns of meaning that are intended (Jensen, 2000). Therefore, students must have a clear understanding of what they are expected to learn (learning standards) within the integrated activity. For young students, the standards may be rewritten and presented using simple terminology.

Plan Assessment: Evidence of Learning

Student assessment in an integrated setting reflects the best assessment practices that occur in other settings. The teacher constantly refers to the standards and performance descriptors when developing the assessments. Scoring rubrics and expectations for performance are developed at this stage. Care must be taken to ensure that the performance standards are being assessed, not the activity itself.

At the conclusion of the lesson, the assessment results are compiled, analyzed, and used to determine student strengths and weaknesses and plan further instruction. In this way, students are provided with the reinforcement and practice they need to meet the standards. If the data show that most students are not meeting a particular standard, it may be because the lesson did not present the right emphasis or focus. The lesson plan should be reviewed and appropriate adjustments made to strengthen student learning.

Develop the Integrated Lesson Design

In planning integrated instruction, appropriate teaching strategies and learning activities are developed that are directly connected to the learning standards. The number of learning standards included in a lesson varies with the level of maturity and capabilities of the students and the expertise and confidence of the teacher.

An overview plan for integrated instruction for an intermediate level class is shown in Figure 2.4. In this plan, language arts standards related to reading, speaking, and writing are included along with science standards related to characteristics of wolves and the ecosystem in which they live. The planning overview is not the lesson plan; it provides the learning standards from which lesson plans are developed. The overview guides the development of specific lessons and assignments.

An example of an integrated instructional plan for an intermediate level class is shown in Figure 2.5. The instructional plan incorporates the learning standards into a lesson plan. The components of the plan include (a) the skills, concepts, strategies, or processes that students are expected to learn; (b) the teaching strategies and student activities that are the vehicle for learning; (c) how students will be grouped for learning; (d) materials and resources to be used; and (e) how assessment of learning will be carried out. In this sample plan, the assessment of student learning includes a written report that is to be scored with a rubric. An example of the Report Writing Assignment for this lesson is shown in Figure 2.6. The associated scoring rubric is shown in Figure 2.7.

An example of an integrated lesson plan for primary level students is shown in Figures 2.8 and 2.9. Integrated Instruction: Overview of Learning Standards (Figure 2.8) shows the major learning theme, specific topic, and performance descriptors for each of the content areas that is included. It is not necessary to include all content areas. There should be a logical connection among the integrated areas. Integrated Instruction Plan (Figure 2.9) contains the specific skills, concepts, strategies, and processes to be taught. It also shows the teaching strategies, class grouping arrangements, materials, and assessment. The column at the far right shows the actual learning standards that are addressed in this lesson. Certainly other standards could be incorporated into this lesson, but consideration must be given to the amount of time for the lesson as well as the complexity of planning. Starting with just a few standards and working these into meaningful learning activities helps to ensure that the standards are taught.

Integrated Instruction: Overview of Learning Standards

Major Learning Theme or Big Idea: Interdependence of living things and the environment

Specific Topic: Wolves and their environment

Reading Performance Descriptors

1. Recognize compare/contrast text structure as embedded in informational text.
2. Recognize descriptive text structure.
3. Use context to determine word meanings: *habitats, regurgitate, prey.*
4. Use reference material (Internet) to obtain information.

Listening/Speaking Performance Descriptors

1. Speak clearly and precisely using appropriate volume.
2. Use eye contact when speaking.

Physical Development Performance Descriptors

None applicable

Mathematics Performance Descriptors

None applicable

Writing Performance Descriptors

1. Use report-writing format to present information related to the topic of study.
2. Present information in a clear and coherent manner.
3. Use correct spelling and mechanics.
4. Use computer program to generate a report on wolves.

Science Performance Descriptors

1. Describe the organized units in which wolves live.
2. Describe the communication system used by wolves.
3. Describe the importance of cooperation in hunting.
4. Explain why wolves are an endangered species.
5. Debate the issue of reintroducing wolves into the northwestern United States.
6. Explain the ecosystem of the tundra and how wolves are part of the system.
7. Recognize vocabulary associated with the lesson (*tundra, ecosystem, species*).

Social Studies Performance Descriptors

1. Describe the characteristics, location, and extent of the tundra.
2. Locate wolf habitats on a world map.

Fine Arts Standards

1. Research artistic renderings of wolves. Compare to photos of real wolves (optional).

Figure 2.4   Integrated Instruction: Overview of Learning Standards

Integrated Instruction Plan

Interdependence of Living Things and the Environment: Wolves and Their Environment

Learning Standards (skills, concepts, strategies, processes)	Teaching Strategies/ Student Activities	Student Grouping Arrangement	Materials and Resources	Assessment
• Survey and predict what a reading text selection is about • Recognize text structure: (1) Compare/contrast is the minor text structure for gray wolf, arctic wolf, tundra wolf (2) Description used as major structure • Develop vocabulary specific to a unit of study: 1. *habitats* pp. 3, 14 2. *regurgitate* p. 6 3. *prey* pp. 7, 8–9, 11 4. Others to be determined during class discussion	Ask about prior experiences and background knowledge of wolves. Fill in Anticipation Guide worksheet. Preview selection. (Book Walk) Predict the kind of information that will be learned from reading this text.	Whole class	Text: *Call of the Wolves* (Berger) Anticipation Guide worksheet	Observe students to determine on-task behavior, level of text difficulty.
• Research and organize major concepts: 1. Wolves live in organized units. 2. Wolves have a communication system. 3. Wolves cooperate in hunting. 4. Wolves are an endangered species. 5. Wolves are part of the tundra ecosystem.	Independent reading of text Discussion of text structure and context clues	Individual support group for less able readers Whole class	Text	Continue observation of students. Use observational checklist.
	Concept mapping (after reading selection)	Small groups (jigsaw approach)	Chart paper, transparencies, markers	Student presentations of concept maps (Use speaking rubric to assess.)
• Organize information in report format • Write to convey information (expository)	Report related to major concepts, i.e., compare and contrast wolf and human communication. Review rubric for informational reports.		Tech connect: Research Internet resources Presentation software program	Written report (Use existing rubric for informational reports.)
Conclusions/Connections/Reflections • Speak clearly and distinctly to an audience. • Discuss prior and newly acquired information.	Revisit Anticipation Guide Discuss similarities and differences: *Julie of the Wolves, Call of the Wild*	Whole group	Discussion questions	Share reports with other classes, parent.

Figure 2.5 Integrated Instruction Plan: Interdependence of Living Things and the Environment: Wolves and Their Environment

Report Writing Assignment

Research your topic:

1. Get to know your topic. Sources of information are books, the Internet, videos, and encyclopedias.

2. As you learn about your topic, write down important information and facts. Keep your information organized according to topics you may want to include in your report such as habitat, characteristics, unusual features, and so forth.

3. Review the Report Writing Rubric.

4. Organize your information and write an outline for a rough draft.

Write the report:

1. Review your outline.

2. Write an introduction that tells the purpose of your report. This includes the main ideas you will write in your report.

3. Include at least five important ideas that cover your topic. Each important idea will be one section of your report.

4. Include illustrations, pictures, or other graphics that help explain your topic.

5. Write a closing that tells what was learned in the report.

6. Check spelling and grammar.

7. Use a word-processing program or write your report neatly.

8. Include at least five references that you used in your report. Use the bibliography format described in class. (See the reference information folder in the class library.)

9. Put your report into a report folder and put your title on the front.

Suggested Key Ideas for Animal Reports:

1. Name
   What is the common name and the scientific name of the animal? What does the scientific name mean? What kind of animal is it (mammal, reptile, bird, insect, etc.)?

2. Appearance
   What does the animal look like? Describe the animal: size, weight, body covering, teeth, tail, legs, claws, eyes, etc. This would be a good place to include an illustration or picture.

3. Diet
   What does the animal eat? Where does it find its food?

4. Habitat
   In what type of biome does the animal live? In what part of the world does the animal live?

5. Enemies
   What enemies does the animal have? How does it protect itself? Is it an endangered species?

6. Special information
   Is there something else about this animal that people should know? Are there stories, myths, and legends about this animal?

Figure 2.6   Report Writing Assignment

Report Writing Rubric

	Attempted 1	Developing 2	Developed 3	Accomplished 4
INTRODUCTION	Introduction is missing or disorganized.	Introduction is weak. The purpose of the report must be inferred.	Introduction states the purpose of the report.	Introduction is interesting and clearly describes the purpose of the report.
ORGANIZATION	The report is messy or confusing.	The report has most components but lacks order.	The report has all components but may not follow a logical sequence.	The report components are clearly presented, interesting, and related to the topic. Transitions are used effectively. There is a flow and logical order.
INFORMATION and DETAILS	Information and details are sketchy.	Information and details are limited and may not strongly connect to the main ideas.	Information and details are adequate to describe the main ideas. Connections to the main idea are logical.	Information and details are extensive, logical, interesting, and well thought out.
CLOSING	Closing is missing. The report ends abruptly.	Closing is attempted but is incomplete.	Closing provides a conclusion or summarizes major key ideas without being overly lengthy.	Closing is an appropriate and interesting summary of major key ideas and conclusions.
VOCABULARY	Vocabulary is stilted and restricted.	Vocabulary is narrow and simple. Few topic-related words are used.	Vocabulary is descriptive. Topic-related words are used.	Vocabulary is expressive and descriptive. Topic-related words are used extensively.
SPELLING and GRAMMAR	Major errors in spelling and grammar that detract from meaning are present.	Spelling and grammar are inconsistent but interpretable.	Very few errors in spelling and grammar are noted.	Spelling and grammar are used correctly.
REFERENCES	No references are listed.	References are attempted but incomplete.	References are appropriate; correct format is used.	References are extensive and appropriate; correct format is used.
APPEARANCE	Carelessly done.	Report is neatly done but shows limited attention to format. There are few illustrations.	Report follows correct format, contains illustrations, and is bound in a report booklet.	Report is creative, follows the correct format, contains illustrations and/or graphics, and is bound in a report booklet.

Figure 2.7   Report Writing Rubric

Integrated Instruction: Overview of Learning Standards

Major Learning Theme or Big Idea: Living things and the environment

Specific Topic: Bears live in different environments

Reading Performance Descriptors

1B1b Identify genre forms
2A1b Classify literary works as fiction or nonfiction
1B1a Establish purpose, make predictions
1C1a Use information to form questions and verify predictions
1A1a Apply word analysis skills
1A1b Use context clues and prior knowledge
1C1c Make comparisons across reading selections
2B1a Connect reading to own experience and communicate this to others

Writing Performance Descriptors

3A1 Construct complete sentences using standard conventions

Science Performance Descriptors

Science Standard 12.B
Know and apply concepts that describe how living things interact with each other and their environment.
Benchmark 12.B.1a
Describe and compare characteristics of living things in relationship to their environments.

Listening/Speaking Performance Descriptors

None applicable

Social Studies Performance Descriptors

None applicable

Physical Development Performance Descriptors

None applicable

Fine Arts Performance Descriptors

None applicable

Mathematics Performance Descriptors

None applicable

Figure 2.8 Integrated Instruction: Overview of Learning Standards

Integrated Instruction Plan

Primary Level: Living Things and the Environment: Bears Live in Different Environments

Learning Standards (skills, concepts, strategies, processes)	Teaching Strategies or Methods	Class Grouping	Materials	Assessment	Illinois Standards/ Benchmarks Connection
• Recognize nonfiction text structure	Describe type of text (reading for information, nonfiction)	Whole group	Book: *Black Bears*		1B1b Identify genre forms 2A1b Classify literary works as fiction or nonfiction
• Use prediction	Book Walk, discussion, and/or KWL related to content	Whole group			1B1a Establish purpose, make predictions 1C1a Use information to form questions and verify predictions
Become familiar with new vocabulary: in text: *berries, caves* Other vocabulary: *hibernate, dangerous, real, pretend*	Introduce words through picture clues and discussion	Whole group			1A1a Apply word analysis skills 1A1b Use context clues and prior knowledge
• Major content concepts: 1. Habitat of black bears 2. Characteristics of black bears 3. Differences between real bears and pretend bears 4. Comparison of black bears and polar bears	Guided reading or teacher read aloud and discussion	Small group		Fill in Information Map	1C1c Make comparisons across reading selections
	Discuss real and pretend bears – Plan a "Teddy Bear Day"	Whole group	*Three Bears, The Bears' Picnic,* or other bear fiction		2B1a Connect reading to own experience and communicate this to others
	Tech Connect: Demonstrate Internet search for information on bears. List facts found.				3A1 Construct complete sentences using standard conventions
	Create a "bear book," i.e., *Where's the Bear?*	Individual		Write a 3- to 5-sentence paragraph related to black bears.	Science Standard 12 B Know and apply concepts that describe how living things interact with each other and their environment. Benchmark 12.B.1a Describe and compare characteristics of living things in relationship to their environments.

Figure 2.9 Integrated Instruction Plan: Primary Level: Living Things and the Environment: Bears Live in Different Environments

USING THE INTEGRATED INSTRUCTIONAL DESIGN PLANNING GUIDE

Planning integrated instruction includes the same components as basic lesson planning. The difference, however, is in the number and type of learning standards that are taught. Because of this, it is critical that teachers remain focused on the standards as planning progresses. It may be tempting to focus on activities, but it is the learning standards that lead the instructional planning process. The Integrated Instructional Design Planning Guide (Figure 2.10) is a tool to assist teachers in thinking through all the components of effective integrated lessons. It is composed of three sections: Section 1: Desired Results—Standards and Performance Descriptors; Section 2: Assessment—Evidence of Learning; and Section 3: Lesson Design. Each of these three sections includes three columns: "Planning Questions and Decisions," "Information and Data Sources," and "Notes and Comments." The Planning Questions and Decisions column poses a series of key questions to guide and stimulate thinking during the planning process. The Information and Data Sources column lists the types of resources and data sources that will facilitate answering the questions in column one. The Notes and Comments column provides information that will further clarify and assist in answering the questions in column one. An example of a planning guide developed by a fifth grade teaching team is shown in Figure 2.11. The team used the guide to structure their discussion and begin their planning.

Teachers who have little or no previous experience in planning integrated instruction will find the planning guide a supportive scaffold in their initial efforts. Novice and preservice teachers will find it helpful to follow all the steps in the planning guide. As a result, subsequent planning will be easier. Experienced teachers with an understanding of integrated instructional design may find that they need only review the questions and activities and focus on those areas that will enhance their planning efforts. Planning integrated instruction involves the following steps:

1. Read the planning guide in its entirety.

It is good practice to become thoroughly familiar with the planning guide before using it. This will save time in the long run. Get the big picture in mind before filling in the details.

2. Think through each of the sections of the planning guide.

Begin with Section 1: Desired Results—Standards and Performance Descriptors. Think about the questions in column one and write down your thoughts and ideas. Consult the data and information sources suggested in column two and note the reminders and supplemental information in column three. Add notes and comments of your own that will be helpful in subsequent planning. Planning questions may be deleted or added to fit your situation. Continue through Section 2: Assessment—Evidence of Learning and Section 3: Lesson Design.

3. Synthesize information.

The thinking process described above provides a great deal of information which now must be synthesized into a coherent plan. Begin your plan with the Integrated Instruction: Overview of Learning Standards (reproducible at the end of this chapter). Then use the Integrated Instruction Plan form to write the specifics of the lesson.

SUMMARY OF GENERAL PLANNING STEPS FOR INTEGRATED LEARNING

The Integrated Instructional Design Planning Guide contains the detailed description of how to plan for integrated instruction. The steps below are a general outline of the process.

1. Think through the process of integrated instruction using the Integrated Instructional Design Planning Guide (Figure 2.10 and the second reproducible).

2. Determine the rationale for using an integrated learning approach.

3. Discuss and select an integration model (Figure 2.1).

4. Develop a Curriculum Calendar Map (Figure 2.2).

5. Align topics of study on the Curriculum Calendar Map (Figure 2.3).

6. Document learning standards and connections on the Integrated Instruction: Overview of Learning Standards form (p. 58).

7. Develop the Integrated Instruction Plan (Figures 2.5 and 2.9 and the third reproducible).

8. Determine and develop specific lesson plans as needed (see Chapter 1).

REFLECTIVE PRACTICE: INNER DIALOGUE

Merely following an outline or filling in a template is not sufficient to develop expertise in planning powerful lessons. Planning is a metacognitive, reflective process in which the teacher thinks, reflects, adjusts, redirects, fiddles, and fine-tunes the various components until a powerful lesson emerges. When reflection is an intrinsic part of the instructional planning process and teachers take time to analyze their planning efforts, they learn through their experiences, and future planning becomes more effective and efficient.

What Costa (1991) calls "inner dialogue" is essential to professional growth, change, and improvement. Use the Inner Dialogue page (Figure 2.12) to reflect on planning actions, attempts, and results of using the Integrated Instructional Design. Be open-minded but skeptical. Consider pros and cons, benefits, and challenges. Look beyond what was accomplished to why and how it was accomplished.

INTEGRATED INSTRUCTIONAL DESIGN PLANNING GUIDE

SECTION 1: Desired Results—Standards and Performance Descriptors

Integrated lessons are grounded on standards and performance descriptors. Use these questions to plan an integrated instructional design.

Planning Questions and Decisions	Information and Data Sources	Notes and Comments
1. How and why will teaching and learning be more effective if learning standards are integrated within lessons rather than taught separately?	Review professional literature on integrated instruction as it relates to the district curriculum, state standards, student needs based on test data (formal and informal), school improvement goals, and district and school goals.	It is important to have a rationale for integrated instruction that is clearly communicated to parents and other stakeholders.
2. What connections exist among the learning standards?	Refer to the curriculum calendar map (Figures 2.2, 2.3).	Determine what relationships already exist among the curriculum areas by constructing a curriculum map. Don't try to force standards to fit into an integrated design. There should be a natural, easy coordination.
3. How will learning standards be organized and documented?	Refer to the Integrated Instruction: Overview of Learning Standards reproducible.	Construct a graphic showing the relationships of the learning standards across the content areas.
4. Which standards are higher priorities than others?	Review student strengths and weaknesses as shown in assessment data.	Determine the level of importance of the standards. Higher priority standards should be given greater instructional time.

Figure 2.10   Integrated Instructional Design Planning Guide

SECTION 2: Assessment—Evidence of Learning

Student assessment must be aligned to what students should know and be able to do as defined in the learning standards and performance descriptors. Use these questions to plan assessment procedures for integrated instruction.

Planning Questions and Decisions	Information and Data Sources	Notes and Comments
1. How will students demonstrate their learning?	Review any required and optional assessments. See curriculum resources and best practice information related to various types of assessment.	Refer to standards and performance descriptors as you finalize decisions regarding assessment. Assessments must be valid and reliable indicators of students' performance.
2. What assessment materials are available and what materials need to be developed?	Review rubrics and assessments in district curriculum guides, teacher manuals, and other sources.	Align the assessment to the learning standards. Students should only be responsible for what they have been taught.
3. How will the assessment results be evaluated or scored?	If available, consider electronic scoring of selected response assessments. Review existing assessments and rubrics.	Select or design needed rubrics or scoring keys. Consider student participation in design of rubrics.
4. How will assessment results be reported?	Review student report card format to be sure that any integrated assessments can be reported.	Consider report cards, grading scale, portfolios, and other means. If a schoolwide grading scale is required, align rubric levels with the grading scale.
5. What further practice and follow-up assessment can be provided for students who fall below expectations?	Alternative test forms may be available for retesting.	It is efficient to have a file of alternative test forms available to use when needed. Consider creating or selecting alternative tests as the lesson is developed.
6. How will assessment results be used?	District policies and handbooks related to assessment use. See *Student Evaluation Standards* (Joint Committee on Standards for Educational Evaluation, 2003).	Use assessment results to determine student strengths and weaknesses and plan the next lessons.

Figure 2.10 (Continued)

SECTION 3: Lesson Design

Use these questions to plan an integrated instructional design.

Planning Questions and Decisions	Information and Data Sources	Notes and Comments
1. What are the specific learning standards to be taught?	Use the Integrated Instruction Overview of Learning Standards form to document the learning standards that will be taught.	Be sure to align the learning standards to the activities as shown on the Integrated Instruction Planner. Redundancies should be noted and eliminated.
2. What is a motivating opening for the unit?		Create interest and anticipation in the unit.
3. What are some possible teaching/learning strategies?	Curriculum guides, teacher manuals, professional literature, best practices information, etc., are sources of information for teaching and learning activities.	Use the Integrated Instruction Plan form as you consider the planning questions in column one.
4. What materials are needed to support and enhance learning?	Check the materials and resources available through the school, library, and community. Students may be asked to bring in related materials if needed and if they have access to them. Check internet sources and software programs.	
5. What opportunities will students have to reflect on their learning?		Remember to provide time for reflection and processing throughout the unit—not just at the end.
6. How will students be grouped for instructional activities?		If small group instruction is planned, consider how this will occur—needs-based, interest-based, other.
7. What minilessons will be conducted?	See the Lesson Plan form.	Even when learning standards are integrated, it is necessary to develop specific lesson plans for day-to-day teaching. These lessons contain all the components of the Basic Lesson Design (Chapter 1). • Motivating opening • Teaching/learning strategies • Materials and resources • Closure • Student groups • Follow-up practice • Assessment
8. What forms of practice will be used?		Students may be grouped to address common needs.
9. How long will this unit take?	Calendar of school events, holidays, curriculum pacing guides, and testing schedules are sources of information for scheduling.	Develop a specific organized calendar and schedule for the activities.
10. Are there any foreseeable pitfalls in this lesson?		Think ahead to avoid potential difficulties.
11. What will I do if the lesson/unit doesn't work out?		A fallback plan is helpful to avoid potential chaos.

Figure 2.10 (Continued)

INTEGRATED INSTRUCTIONAL DESIGN: EXAMPLE FROM A GRADE 5 TEAM

SECTION 1: Desired Results—Standards and Performance Descriptors

1. How and why will teaching and learning be more effective if learning standards are integrated within lessons rather than taught separately?

We have a modified departmentalized arrangement for Grade 5 students. According to our curriculum calendar map, it seems we have been teaching the same concepts in several different classes. If we plan together, we can eliminate this redundancy and have time for teaching other concepts. We also noticed there are different writing rubrics in use. We want reading and writing skills to be consistently taught in all curriculum areas. Students will experience connections among the content areas and be involved in using information across the curriculum. This approach will strengthen their learning and make it more meaningful. We need to get coordinated!

2. What connections exist among the learning standards?

The standards we have identified are from reading, writing, listening/speaking, science, social studies, and fine arts. At this time, we did not see a connection to any math standards or physical education standards but would like to build other units to incorporate these areas also. We as teachers are beginning to build connections in our minds. Perhaps this is the first step to helping our students do the same.

3. How will learning standards be organized and documented?

We are going to use the Integrated Instruction: Overview of Learning Standards as a starting point (Figure 2.4 and the first reproducible). We discussed how we would use this tool to provide our students with an overview of what they will learn. We might set up an assembly arrangement to kick this off.

4. Which learning standards have a higher priority than others? How will priorities be accommodated?

The way we planned this out, all the standards are important. Students will need some out-of-class time to work on their computer reports, so we will need to plan for that. Otherwise, too much class time will be used.

Figure 2.11   Integrated Instructional Design: Example From Grade 5 Team

INTEGRATED INSTRUCTIONAL DESIGN: EXAMPLE FROM A GRADE 5 TEAM

SECTION 2: Assessment—Evidence of Learning			
1. How will students be assessed?	**2. How will the assessment be scored?**	**3. How will the assessment results be used?**	**4. How will the assessment be reported?**
a. Concept map related to wolves (group task).	a. Develop rubric for concept map activity. Distribute to students when assignment is given.	a. Feedback for students on their work as a group.	a. Group scores based on rubric.
b. Concept map presentation to class (all members of group will have a part).	b. Speaking/listening rubric to assess presentation of information.	b. Feedback for students and teacher on how speaking/listening skills are used.	b. Individual scores based on rubric.
c. Written reflection by each student on their participation in the group's work.	c. No scoring—comments only.	c. Feedback for teacher on how students participated in the group work.	c. Comments from the teacher.
Selected response test (20 items).	Answer key (20 items, 5 points each). Sign up to use Scantron for scoring.	Determine which students need reinforcement of factual information. Students make corrections as necessary. Include results in quarterly report card grade for social studies.	Go over test items with students. Grades will be determined according to the schoolwide grading scale.
Written report—specific topic related to wolves selected by each student.	Writing rubric (district).	The rubric will provide feedback to the student. A total of 10 points for this assignment will be included in the quarterly report card grade for written communication.	Copy of rubric showing performance level will be returned to students. Teacher comments will be included as appropriate.
Report—group task. Students will use information from their individual reports to create a computer-generated presentation.	Rubric on presentation of reports.	Feedback for students and teacher on how students worked as a group. A total of 10 points for this assignment will be included in the quarterly report card grade for oral communication.	Copy of rubric for each group will be scored. Teacher comments will be included.
Portfolios—All assessments above will be included with an explanation of the learning standards included in each one.	Rubric developed by teacher and students.	Feedback for students, teachers, and parents on group and individual participation in this unit.	Students will share portfolios with parents.

Figure 2.11 (Continued)

INTEGRATED INSTRUCTIONAL DESIGN: EXAMPLE FROM A GRADE 5 TEAM

SECTION 3: Lesson Design

1. What are the specific learning standards to be taught?

The major learning of this unit is interdependence of living things and the environment. The learning standards cover reading, writing, listening/speaking, science, and social studies. The Integrated Instruction Plan (Figure 2.5 and the reproducible, p. 61) contains the specific list of all the standards.

2. What is a motivating opening for the unit?

All classes will attend the opening activity where the learning standards, purpose, and overview of activities will be described. (Parents could be invited to attend the opening.) Later students will convene in their teams to discuss what they already know about the topic and preview some of the resources they will use.

3. What are some possible teaching/learning strategies?

Cooperative activities will be balanced with independent activities. Some whole-group instruction will be necessary. Guided reading strategies may be used with students who need more support.

4. What materials are needed to support and enhance learning?

Numerous trade books have been preselected and will be available for student use. Students will have opportunities to use the Internet for further research. Presentational software will be used to generate reports.

5. What opportunities will students have to reflect on their learning?

Students will revisit the anticipation guide filled out at the beginning of their study of wolves. They will discuss similarities and differences of fiction and nonfiction selections on wolves.

6. How will students be grouped?

There are four classrooms included in this unit. Two teachers will team teach their groups. All students will be brought together in the library for the presentations on the last three days.

7. What minilessons will be conducted?

- ✓ How to use presentational software (all students)
- ✓ Compare/contrast text structure in reading and writing (all students)
- ✓ Word study and vocabulary (group based on need)

8. What forms of follow-up practice will be used?

Students who have difficulty with reading vocabulary or report writing will be grouped together for additional support lessons relating to these skills.

9. How long will this unit take?

The study will begin on March 4 and continue for 10 days. Students will work on this project for approximately two hours per day. The teachers will schedule mutually convenient times. The amount of time may vary depending on how the students progress. We will develop a written schedule so everyone knows what and when various activities happen.

10. Are there any foreseeable pitfalls in this lesson?

With all this activity going on, some students may be distracted or off task. Also, some students may not participate fully in the cooperative groups. We'll have to monitor closely and facilitate and model appropriate learning behaviors. If necessary, we could devote a practice period to role-playing cooperative group behavior.

11. What will I do if the lesson/unit doesn't work out?

Back to the drawing board! We could survey students to get some feedback from them. We're committed to making this work.

Figure 2.11 (Continued)

Inner Dialogue

Reflect on the planning process to deepen your understanding. Keep your notes and refer to them when you plan again.

This is what I did in the planning process.	This is what I think about it and how I might change or modify it.
Some new learning	
Some benefits	
Some challenges	

Figure 2.12   Inner Dialogue

INTEGRATED INSTRUCTION: OVERVIEW OF LEARNING STANDARDS

Major Learning Theme or Big Idea

Specific Topic

Reading Performance Descriptors

Writing Performance Descriptors

Listening/Speaking Performance Descriptors

Science Performance Descriptors

Physical Development Performance Descriptors

Social Studies Performance Descriptors

Mathematics Performance Descriptors

Fine Arts Performance Descriptors

INTEGRATED INSTRUCTIONAL DESIGN: PLANNING QUESTIONS AND DECISIONS

Desired Results	1. How and why will teaching and learning be more effective if learning standards are integrated within lessons rather than taught separately?
	2. What connections exist among the learning standards?
	3. How will learning standards be organized and documented?
	4. Which learning standards have a higher priority than others? How will priorities be accommodated?
Assessment—Evidence of Learning	5. How will students be assessed?
	6. How will assessments be scored?
	7. How will assessment results be used?
	8. How will assessment results be reported?

(Continued)

(Continued)

Lesson Design	9. What are the specific learning standards to be taught?
	10. What is a motivating opening for the unit/lesson?
	11. What are some possible teaching/learning strategies?
	12. What materials are needed to support and enhance learning?
	13. What opportunities will students have to reflect on their learning?
	14. How will students be grouped?
	15. What minilessons will be conducted?
	16. What forms of follow-up practice will be used?
	17. How long will the lesson/unit take?
	18. Are there any foreseeable pitfalls in this lesson?
	19. What will I do if the lesson/unit does not work out?

INTEGRATED INSTRUCTION PLAN

Learning Standards (skills, concepts, strategies, processes)	Teaching Strategies/ Student Activities	Student Grouping Arrangement	Materials and Resources	Assessment
Closing/Connections/ Reflections				

Differentiated Instructional Design

3

Anyone who spends even a short time in a classroom sees that students differ not only in physical appearance but also in how they learn, their interests, their prior experiences, and their cognitive strengths and weaknesses. These differences become even more pronounced as students advance through the grades. A "one-size-fits-all" model of instruction, therefore, cannot possibly reach all students in a classroom. "That students differ may be inconvenient, but it is inescapable" (Sizer, 1999, p. 6).

Differentiated instruction as it is practiced today differs from past approaches that attempted to reduce the range of student differences through pull-out programs, ability grouping, tracking, and retention. These approaches sorted students according to ability with usually no accommodation for how they learned. Generally, lower ability students were taught with lower level textbooks and materials, and higher ability students were taught with higher level textbooks and materials. Research on these types of ability grouping programs has been generally unfavorable (Good & Brophy, 1997; Oakes, 1988; Slavin, 1987; Zemelman, Daniels, & Hyde, 1993). Differentiated instruction as it is practiced today is quite different from past approaches.

> *Differentiated instruction is a teaching approach that provides a variety of learning options to accommodate differences in how students learn.*

THE MANY FACETS OF DIFFERENTIATED INSTRUCTION

Differentiated instruction is a teaching approach that provides a variety of learning options to accommodate differences in how students learn. Some differences that impact learning are related to the student's background knowledge and experience, instructional strengths and weaknesses, learning preferences and modalities, cognitive levels, and personal interests. While it may not be possible to accommodate all the unique characteristics of students in a classroom, some accommodations through differentiated instruction are not only possible but necessary. According to Csikszentmihalyi (1990), a learner reaches his or her fullest capacity when a task is at an optimal level—neither too difficult nor too simple. When the learner's mental and emotional focus are linked together in learning, a state of "flow" occurs that enhances and sustains learning (Goleman, 1995). It is this state of flow that teachers try to create by providing differentiated activities that will challenge and motivate learners.

Background Knowledge

Teachers help students to make sense of learning by connecting new learning to what is already known.

Students who have a rich background of experiences and are able to connect new experiences into patterns of meaning seem to learn and retain concepts better than those who do not (Caine & Caine, 1991; Jensen, 2000). Teachers help students to make sense of learning by connecting new learning to what is already known. When students know very little about a topic, it is important to build the background that will enable them to benefit from instruction. When students have extensive knowledge of a topic, instruction should enrich and extend what they already know.

Teachers use various types of assessment to determine what students already know about a particular topic, such as the following:

- Cloze procedures in which students fill in missing words or phrases

- Pretests related to the topic

- Observation of students as they engage in an activity or discussion related to the topic

- Prewriting or listing all known information about a topic.

Building background information is different from assessing it. When students have little information related to a topic, it is necessary to build background information that will enable them to more fully understand what they are learning. Activities to help students acquire and build their background of information include the following:

- Independent reading about a topic

- Discussing topic-related artifacts

- Developing semantic maps

- Noting similarities and differences among similar topics

- Watching videos that provide in-depth information

- Engaging in direct experiences

- Listening to read-alouds

- Developing graphic organizers

- Learning topic-related vocabulary

Instructional Strengths and Weaknesses

Instructional strengths and weaknesses are determined by assessing what students know and are able to do in relation to the learning standards.

Gardner's Intelligences

Verbal/Linguistic: The ability to use with clarity the core operations of language

Musical/Rhythmic: The ability to use the core set of musical elements

Logical/Mathematical: The ability to use inductive and deductive reasoning, solve abstract problems, and understand complex relationships

Visual/Spatial: The ability to perceive the visual world accurately and recreate one's visual experiences

Naturalist: The ability to survive in and adapt to one's own environment by understanding nature and all of its elements

Bodily/Kinesthetic: The ability to control and interpret body motions, manipulate physical objects, and establish harmony between the body and mind

Interpersonal: The ability to get along with, interact with, work with, and motivate others toward a common goal

Intrapersonal: The ability to form an accurate model of oneself and to use that model to operate effectively in life

---

Figure 3.1   Gardner's Intelligences

A learning profile obtained through various assessments shows areas of weakness and the skills, concepts, and/or processes that need to be further developed. The learning profile will also show instructional strengths that can be extended or expanded. Assessments used to determine what students know and can do are often in the form of a pencil-and-paper test; however, observation of student performance, evaluation of artifacts (the work the student produces), and performance-based assessments are also useful tools to determine students' abilities.

Multiple Intelligences

Consideration of instructional needs alone does not provide all the information necessary from which to develop instructional activities. Effective instruction combines what students learn with how they learn. In the past, intelligence or IQ was examined in an attempt to determine the strength of a student's ability to learn. In *Frames of Mind*, Howard Gardner (1983) questions the view of intelligence as a single entity and theorizes the existence of several intellectual strengths or competences within an individual. Gardner recognizes eight intelligences, which are briefly described in Figure 3.1. This summary should not be considered a complete description of Gardner's theory, which is far more complex than outlined here. For a complete discussion of Gardner's theory see *Frames of Mind* (Basic Books, 1983).

Students who have a proclivity toward one of these "intelligences" will feel comfortable and confident when participating in activities that involve its use. Therefore, it makes sense to provide students with activities that will allow them to use their preferred intelligence to perform at their best.

Learning Modalities

Educators have long known that learning *modalities*—auditory, visual, kinesthetic, and tactile—influence how students learn. Simply put, visual learners benefit from graphic representations, auditory learners benefit from aural representations, kinesthetic learners benefit from bodily involvement activities, and tactile learners benefit from touching and feeling shapes, forms, and textures (Sprenger, 1999).

Teachers routinely use visual aids such as posters, charts, and models to accompany lessons. They capitalize on students' auditory strengths through auditory input of recordings, "talking toys," conversation, discussion, songs, and dialogue. They provide activities in which students build or construct a physical representation of something they are learning about (e.g., water cycle, bridges, story elements, skeletal system). They provide movement activities that depict some idea or concept such as a dance or physical movement to reinforce multiplication facts. And they provide lesson materials made of special textures (sandpaper, velvet, plastic, rice, pasta, cereal) and shapes that can be manipulated and touched. A variety of activities helps to ensure that all learning modalities are included throughout the school year.

An individual's predominant learning modality does not negate the presence of the other modalities. For this reason, teachers find it beneficial to provide multimodal activities throughout their lessons.

Types of Thinking

Types of thinking may be categorized as literal, relational, transformational, and extensional. *Literal* thinking involves recall of facts and information that have been explicitly provided. Literal learning tasks ask students to name, tell, match, or repeat explicitly provided information.

Tasks that require *relational* thinking ask students to predict, compare, contrast, or explain how information from one or more sources is connected. Prior knowledge is often used as a source of information in relational thinking.

Transformational thinking involves transcribing or applying learning in a different way. Dramatization, diagramming, graphing, and rewriting are examples of transformational tasks.

Extensional thinking is used as students produce, develop, or design an original product or otherwise use their learning in a unique way. Extensional thinking is a creative process that may involve all other forms of thinking: literal, relational, and transformational. It is a coming together of all the relevant knowledge, skills, and processes to create an original concept, process, or product.

It is convenient to categorize types of thinking to plan appropriate instructional activities; however, it is important to know that types of thinking are not necessarily used separately but more often overlap and are used simultaneously by students in learning situations (Good & Brophy, 1997). The intent is not to isolate types of thinking into discrete categories but to realize that thinking occurs along a continuum. Learners engage in thinking that ranges from simple recall to complex abstract levels (Bloom, 1984; see Chapter 1 for further discussion on types of thinking).

Personal Interests

Students develop interests in a particular topic for a variety of reasons. Some interests are fleeting; some last a lifetime. Regardless of what or why, interests do motivate and sustain learning. Teachers who allow students choices and opportunities to select learning activities capitalize on personal interests that lead students into learning and studying a topic (Diamond & Hopson, 1998).

WHY DIFFERENTIATED INSTRUCTION IS A GOOD IDEA

Support for differentiated instruction is seen in the scientific and medical research on how the brain learns. Computerized axial tomography (CAT) and magnetic resonance imaging (MRI) have produced images that show the brain in action (Sousa, 2005). Brain images show that people with reading problems use different parts of the brain than do those without reading problems. This is a new and rapidly developing science that offers great potential for understanding how the brain learns. Shaywitz and Shaywitz (2004) propose that through this type of diagnosis more effective treatment will be possible. While brain research in itself does not tell us how to teach, it can inform our instructional practices.

Right Amount of Challenge

When students are challenged and engaged in tasks, they become motivated and invested in their learning. Jensen (2000) says that the right amount of challenge is a critical element in learning—too much leads to frustration, too little leads to boredom. If students in a classroom are all expected to perform the same learning activity, it is likely that some will be frustrated and some will be bored because the level of challenge does not meet their needs. A differentiated instructional plan helps to ensure that students participate in learning activities that are at (or at least close to) their optimal learning level.

A differentiated instructional plan helps to ensure that students participate in learning activities that are at (or at least close to) their optimal learning level.

Transfer of Learning

Activities that help students see connections to real-life situations and apply what they learn to new situations create opportunities for transfer of learning (Fogarty, 1997). *Transfer*, or use of knowledge, skills, and processes in new situations, is perhaps the ultimate goal of education. It matters little if we possess vast amounts of knowledge and information if we cannot use and apply that knowledge.

Students need complex real-life experiences to learn and grow. Simple linear approaches such as those designed to teach isolated skills are not as powerful as those that provide interactive, hands-on activities in which students explore, manipulate, and connect ideas and concepts (Caine & Caine, 1991). An example of a complex activity that asks students to apply what they know

---

Design a CD Cover

A famous music recording company has asked you to design a cover for one of their latest releases. You are to submit your design on graph paper according to the company's directions that are outlined below. Be sure you include all the necessary items in your design.

1. The title should occupy one quarter of the cover.

2. Include all of the following items on the cover and tell what fractional part of the cover each occupies:
   - Titles and descriptions of songs
   - Information about the artist
   - Pictures or graphics

3. Explain in words what fractional part each item is, compared to the whole cover.

Figure 3.2   Design a CD Cover

to solve a problem or perform a task is shown in Figure 3.2. Students must first conceptualize what to do or, in other words, determine what the problem is. They must then call to mind the skills and processes already learned that will help solve the problem. Working through the task, students must continually evaluate their progress and make adjustments accordingly. This metacognitive strategy is critical in accurate problem solving. The solution—the outcome of the task—is judged against criteria (either provided by the teacher or determined by the student).

THE DIFFERENTIATED CLASSROOM

Differentiated instruction may be applied to certain units and lessons, or it may become an overarching philosophy toward which all classroom instruction is geared. Teachers who espouse differentiation strive to create a learning environment in which students' differences are recognized and respected. Students are supported in learning through activities that are at an appropriate level of challenge and interest. Interdependence is balanced with independence. Learning is seen as a goal that may be achieved in a variety of ways.

THE ROLE OF LEARNING STANDARDS IN DIFFERENTIATED INSTRUCTION

Learning standards provide descriptions of what students should know and be able to do. There is a vast amount of information about learning standards available today; state boards of education, professional organizations, and school districts all have developed lists of content area standards. The formats used by different organizations may be different, but the purpose and intent is the same—to provide information on what students should know and be able to do. A sample showing the relationship of standards and performance descriptors

---

Relationship of Standards and Performance Descriptors: Example From Social Studies

Social Studies Learning Standard: Understand and explain basic principles of the United States government.

Performance Descriptors:

1. *List* reasons for forming a government.
2. *Describe* the purpose of the Declaration of Independence.
3. *Describe* the purpose of the United States Constitution.
4. *Compare* the purpose of the United States Constitution and the Constitution of the state of Oregon.
5. *List* the basic rights of citizens provided in the Bill of Rights.
6. *Differentiate* between citizenship by birth and naturalization.
7. *Describe* the responsibilities of adults in maintaining local governments (e.g., voting, serving on community boards, paying taxes, serving on juries).
8. *Defend* (or *debate*) the position that people in a democracy must have freedom of speech, freedom of the press, freedom of religion, and freedom of assembly.

Figure 3.3   Relationship of Standards and Performance Descriptors: Example From Social Studies

is shown in Figure 3.3. The standard is defined in terms of specific performance descriptors, which become the focal point for planning instruction.

While the abundance of standards may seem to make lesson planning an overwhelming task, a closer look reveals similarities and overlapping among the standards. When teachers put learning standards to use in planning instruction, they select the standards their students need to meet. Then they plan instruction focused on those standards.

Standards are central to instructional planning. Inexperienced teachers tend to jump in and begin planning activities—what the students will do. However, before planning the activities, decisions must be made regarding what students will learn—what learning standards are to be addressed. The activities are the *means* to this end.

In a differentiated classroom, students are not learning different things— they are learning the same things differently. Tomlinson (1999) states that all students need the same essential principles and even the same key skills. The way they go about acquiring these principles and skills through various learning activities is what differentiated learning is all about. In planning differentiated instruction, the teacher must first decide what learning standards will be addressed and assessed, next decide the basis for differentiation, and then plan appropriate activities.

In a differentiated classroom, students are not learning different things— they are learning the same things differently.

In a differentiated classroom, students engage in a range of activities based on their instructional needs. Even though students are involved in different learning activities, they still addressing the same learning standards. The challenge to teachers is to know the learning characteristics of their students and plan instruction for optimal learning. Obviously, not all differences in students' learning characteristics can be addressed in all lessons all the time. Effective teachers determine priorities and design instruction based on those priorities.

TEACHING WITH A DIFFERENTIATED APPROACH

The rationale for differentiated instruction is that students will be more engaged in their learning and learn more if instruction is matched to their needs. Students' needs differ, and therefore instruction must likewise differ. In a differentiated classroom, students are grouped for instruction based on common needs. Grouping arrangements are purposeful and efficient. Whole-group, small-group, and individual learning activities are all part of a differentiated classroom. Whole-group instruction is appropriate when common instructional needs arise. Small-group instruction is indicated when the range of needs is too broad to be adequately addressed with the whole group. Individual instruction or reinforcement is planned when a student has a particular need that differs from those of other students or groups. Following is a description of various types of grouping arrangements including whole class, partnering, cooperative learning, student-led discussions, individual projects, and learning centers.

Whole-Class Instruction

There are times when it is appropriate to teach a new concept or introduce a new procedure to all students at the same time. However, even within this context, the teacher may differentiate instruction. For example, during a whole-class discussion or presentation, the teacher may direct a question to a particular student, asking for a restatement, a summarization, a connecting comment, a clarification, a judgment, or evaluation. The level of difficulty of the question is meant to challenge but not overwhelm or discourage the student. All students benefit from being part of this type of lesson, listening to their peers, and responding not only to the teacher but to each other as well.

Partnering

There is a difference between partners working to strengthen each other's learning and peer tutoring, which is designed to strengthen the learning of one of the partners. In the context of a differentiated classroom, partnering is *not* intended as tutoring with one student teaching or testing another but as a mutually beneficial learning activity. When two students work together on a task, they strengthen each other's understanding, reinforce their learning, and share information. Partnered students do not necessarily need to be at the same ability level, but their levels should be close enough so that the activity will be of interest and a challenge to each. For some partner activities, it is helpful to pair a low-ability student with a student of slightly higher ability so that one may serve as a model. Partner work also helps to build the interdependence necessary for working with four or five students in a cooperative group.

Student-Led Discussion Groups

Being a part of a student-led discussion group helps students develop leadership and group participation skills. Groups may be based on students' reading levels when the purpose is to discuss a reading selection they have completed.

Groups also may be based on a particular topic or theme-related reports students have completed. Teaching students to be good participants and leaders is critical to the success of a student-led discussion group. Teacher modeling of how to participate as well as how to lead helps students understand these roles. Initially, it is helpful for the teacher to model good discussion questions and then provide opportunities for students to develop their own questions. Ongoing supervision and support also contributes to successful group interaction.

Cooperative Learning Groups

Positive social interaction enhances learning (Jensen, 2000; Sylwester, 1995). When students participate effectively as members of a group, each contributes to the purpose of the group. The interdependence of the group members impacts the functioning of the group as well as the outcome. Therefore, it is important that students learn how to be effective group participants and group leaders.

The benefits of cooperative learning have been known for many years. Students in cooperative learning settings tend to perform better academically than students taught in individualistic or competitive settings (Johnson & Johnson, 1984). Bellanca and Fogarty (1991) discuss the overwhelming positive research on cooperative learning. "Over and over, with a consistency and reliability remarkable for a school methodology, the studies have demonstrated how and why cooperative learning is one of the most powerful teaching and learning tools available" (p. 242).

The National Reading Panel (2000) report likewise affirms the efficacy of cooperative learning as a reading comprehension strategy. The panel's review of the research concludes that when students listen and discuss and help one another use reading strategies, their comprehension is strengthened (sec. 4, p. 43), and they gain independence and control over their learning as they interact with others (sec. 4, p. 101).

Cooperative learning can offer a real-life aspect to classroom work. In their book on best practices, Zemelman and colleagues (1993) state,

> Every child needn't study every possible topic, and not everyone has to study all the same topics. Indeed, it is good educational practice (and solid preparation for adult life) to be part of a community where tasks and topics are parceled out to work groups, task forces, teams, or committees. (p. 143)

Teachers may "jigsaw" an activity or task into several parts. Groups of students engage in one of the parts and then bring their learning back to the entire group. In this manner, the pieces of the jigsaw puzzle are fit together and students learn from one another.

Individual Learning

Not all classroom activities must be cooperative grouping arrangements. Just as there are valid reasons for cooperative-group activities and whole-group instruction, there are times when students should be allowed to work

---

Create a Math Test

Task Description

Design a math test on multiplication of two-digit numbers by two-digit numbers. Your math test will be taken by other students. Your test should be fair—not too easy and not too hard.

Special Features

Your test should have the following:

✓ 10 computation problems
✓ 5 story problems

   Options:
      Include one problem about time
      Include one problem about money

✓ 1 math writing activity
✓ An answer key on a separate sheet

Wing Dings

You may use the computer to write your test problems.
You may illustrate your story problems.

Timeline and Date Due

You will have five school days to complete your math task.
You may work on your task at home if you wish.

Organization and Storage

Keep your work in your math folder.
Turn in your folder on the date due.

Bonuses

If you finish your math task before the due date, you may

   a. read a book
   b. write in your journal
   c. use the computer for _____
   d. work on your art project
   e. other _____

Figure 3.4   Create a Math Test

---

individually. A student who exhibits an intense interest in exploring a topic from another perspective, has a specialized need that does not "fit" any of the group activities, or simply prefers to work alone should be allowed to do so. Further, all students should be given opportunities to work individually to practice self-reliance and show what they can do on their own. At other times, the choice of working with a group or individually gives students control over how they learn and promotes motivation and independence. All these arrangements have a place in the differentiated classroom.

When students work individually they need precise directions on exactly what they are to accomplish and how they will be assessed. An example of an individual learning activity is shown in Create a Math Test (Figure 3.4). This standards-based activity is designed for students who have mastered two-digit multiplication and are ready to apply and extend what they have learned. The specific features of the assignment are clearly described, and related information is provided on when the assignment is due, where to keep the ongoing work, and what to do when the assignment is completed. The rubric shown in Figure 3.5 provides further clarity and specific expectations for the assignment.

The steps involved in developing an individual learning activity are as follows:

Math Task Rubric				
	Poor 1	**Fair 2**	**Excellent 3**	**Exceptional 4**
Computation Problems	Several of the problems are missing.	Two problems are missing.	One problem is missing.	All problems are stated.
Story Problems	Problems are not clearly stated and show little evidence of mathematical reasoning.	Problems are somewhat clear and show understanding of mathematical concepts.	Problems are clearly stated and show understanding of mathematical concepts.	Problems are well designed, clearly stated, and show an understanding of mathematical concepts.
Writing Activity	The writing activity is missing or very poorly stated.	The writing activity shows some understanding of the mathematical concept.	The writing activity provides all necessary information and is clearly stated.	The writing activity provides all necessary information, is clearly stated, and is interesting.
Neatness and Organization	The assignment is disorganized and is not clearly presented.	There is some organization to the assignment but it has some confusing parts.	The assignment is organized and clear to read.	The assignment is well organized, easy to follow, and presented in an interesting manner.
Directions and Explanations	Directions are missing or very confusing.	Directions may be confusing or have some part missing.	Directions are clearly stated and all parts are explained.	Directions and explanations are clearly stated and are easy to understand and carry out.
Wing Dings (optional)	Attempt was made but was not satisfactorily carried out.	Computer formatting is adequate but contains numerous errors.	Computer formatting is satisfactory.	Computer formatting is appropriate and adds to interest and readability.
	Some attempted illustrations.	Illustrations are minimal and may lack clarity.	Appropriate illustrations are included.	Illustrations are well executed and add interest.

Figure 3.5   Math Task Rubric

1. State the task. Provide explanation as necessary.

2. Outline specific features of the task.

3. Describe "extras" (wing dings)—optional features that the student may include in the project.

4. Specify a timeline and/or date due.

5. Specify where work in progress is to be kept.

6. Provide bonus activities for early completion.

7. Develop a rubric or checklist for performance.

Project Pack Assignment

Name: _____ Starting date: _____

Timeline	Task	Date completed
Day 1	• Read the two books in your pack. • Use the Fact/React Sheet to list at least five things from each book.	
Day 2	Continue your reading.	
Day 3	• Use the recommended Web sites in your pack to continue your exploration of this topic. • Add new information to your Fact/React Sheet.	
Day 4	Continue your Web site exploration.	
Day 5	• Select three most interesting facts from your Fact/React Sheet. • Illustrate this information using large chart paper. Use one paper for each fact.	
Day 6	Continue working on your illustrations.	
Day 7	• Prepare an outline of a brief presentation to the class on your top three facts related to your topic.	

Materials:

1. Book 1
2. Book 2
3. Fact/React Sheet
4. Internet sites list
5. Set of markers
6. Chart paper in materials supply cabinet

Your grade will be based on the following:	
1. The completeness of your Fact/React Sheet, including book and Web site information	10 points
2. The completeness and details in your illustrations	10 points
3. The organization of your outline	5 points
4. Your oral presentation to the class based on the oral presentation rubric	5 points

Figure 3.6 Project Pack Assignment

Another type of individual activity is the Project Pack (Skowron, 2003). The Project Pack Assignment Sheet provides a timeline and a description of day-by-day activities, materials to be used, and how the assignment will be graded. The example shown in Figure 3.6 is a social studies assignment that includes reading two pieces of related text, using Web site information, illustrating pertinent information, and developing an oral report.

Learning Centers

A learning center is a location in the classroom where a small group of students work on an activity as a group project or individually on the same activity. The activity is based on learning standards that students need to meet.

Therefore, the first step in planning a learning center is to define its purpose in terms of learning standards. Students who need additional reinforcement or practice on the learning standard are those who will participate in the learning center. Other learning centers may be established for students to extend and enrich their learning.

Learning centers may be contained in a designated section of the classroom or contained in a bin or box from which students obtain the materials they need to work at their own desk or elsewhere in the classroom. Space is an important consideration in setting up centers and is considered along with the kind of activities students are expected to complete (Diller, 2005).

Learning center activities should be at an appropriate level of challenge yet allow students to complete the task without becoming frustrated because they lack sufficient background or skill to do so. Activities that are too difficult may lead to off task behavior due to frustration; activities that are too easy may lead to off task behavior because of boredom. When the learning center activity involves reading, it is best for text to be at the student's independent reading level. (The generally accepted criteria for independent reading are 99% correct for word accuracy and 90% correct for comprehension accuracy.)

Activities that are too difficult may lead to off task behavior due to frustration; activities that are too easy may lead to off task behavior because of boredom.

Learning center activities may be individual or collaborative. In each case, an appropriate location for the learning center must be considered. Quiet activities should be located where students will not be distracted. Collaborative activities in which students converse with one another and even move about the room are appropriately located away from where others are engaged in instructional and individual work.

One of the most important factors in determining the success of the learning center activity is the clarity of the directions given to the students. It is imperative that students understand what they are to do in order to avoid confusion, off task behavior, and interruptions. Many teachers find it helpful to model the use of the center and engage students in developing learning center rules (Diller, 2003). An easy-to-read directions sheet or poster placed near the learning center serves as a reminder to students of what they are to do. Directions should also include information on what students are to do when they have completed the activity.

The timeline for learning center activities may be a single 20-minute period or several days or even weeks, depending on how long the activities take to complete and the number of students who will use the center. Students may be given a definite time limit or allowed to complete the activity at their own pace. In either case, the teacher specifies the time requirement and makes this known to the students.

Learning centers contain all the materials that students need to complete an assigned task. Replenishing materials may be necessary if several groups of students are expected to use the learning center.

Accountability is feedback on what the student learned and the learning center activity itself. The activity must be worthy of the student's time. It must provide needed practice and help the student in meeting the learning standards. If the activity is worth doing, then a measure of how well the student did it provides feedback on progress toward meeting the learning standard.

Writing Center Plan

Center: Developmental writing

Purpose (learning standard): 3C. Communicate ideas in writing to accomplish a variety of purposes. Develop writing fluency. Use letter and sound information to write words. Use sentence (language) sense to write sentences.

Center location: Writing materials contained on small corner table. Students select materials from center and do written activity at the table.

Center activities:	**Center materials:**
Developmental story writing: Student selects object from the "writing box," draws a picture of it at top of paper, and writes two sentences about it.	Writing box (beanie babies, pictures, Matchbox cars), paper, crayons

Preparation and directions:

1. Look through the writing box for something you like.

2. Take the object, a piece of paper, and a crayon to the table.

3. Draw a picture of the object.

4. Write two sentences that tell about your picture.

5. Put your paper in your work folder.

6. Put all your materials away.

7. Go to the reading rug or the drawing table.

Accountability measures:

Student's picture and sentences; conference with students about stories; whole-group sharing of selected pictures.

Figure 3.7   Writing Center Plan

Accountability of learning center work may be provided through (a) the student's completed assignment, (b) observation during the activity, (c) whole-group sharing of what has been accomplished, or (d) student checklists or assessments.

The learning center schedule is part of the classroom schedule. Scheduling decisions take into account the following: (a) how many students will use the center, (b) how much time will be allowed at the center (timed or untimed use), (c) rotation of groups through the center, and (d) transition time for changing activities.

An example of a learning center plan for developmental writing is shown in Figure 3.7. In this example, the writing center contains the materials the students need to work individually on their own story. Figure 3.8 is an example of a math learning center plan. The Learning Center Plan reproducible (p. 106) is provided for developing other learning center plans.

Math Learning Center Plan

Center: Math

Purpose (learning standard): 6B. Investigate, represent, and solve problems using number facts, operations, and their properties, algorithms, and relationships. Stage C.6. Apply knowledge of basic multiplication facts.

Center location: Materials contained in plastic bin on small corner table. Students select materials from center and do written activity at their own desk or other self-selected location.

Center activities:	**Center materials**
Math problem-solving activities: Students use math kits (activity card, worksheet, and related math manipulatives in a ziplock bag) for problem-solving activities. Students use an answer key to assess their work.	Math kits (plastic ziplock bags), answer key cards, individual math folder

Preparation and directions:

1. Select a math kit from the math center.
2. Take your math kit to your desk or other comfortable place in the classroom.
3. Solve the problem on your math card.
4. Use your worksheet to keep track of your work.
5. Use the answer key to see if you are right.
6. Put your worksheet in your math work folder.
7. Put all materials away.
8. If you have time remaining:
   - work on another math kit
   - read a book
   - (other)

Accountability measures:

Student's math worksheet (in math folder); conference with student regarding math problem; group sharing of math problems

Figure 3.8   Math Learning Center Plan

When teachers initiate learning centers, they make sure students understand the purpose and use of the learning center and that they will be accountable for the work they do in the center. Monitoring and assisting students as they work in centers helps them to become more independent learners. When students are able to work independently in a learning center, constant supervision is no longer necessary, and the teacher may direct her attention to working with other students.

In a well-run differentiated classroom, group assignments are not permanent, especially when achievement level is used as a criterion for grouping. Assignment to low achieving groups is detrimental to learning and often a self-fulfilling prophecy when groups are permanent (Allington, 1991; Opitz, 1997;

Slavin, 1987). The practice of grouping by reading levels should be balanced with flexibility; that is, students should be reassigned to a group based on changing needs. Other activities also should be provided to allow students to interact and learn in groups based on a variety of criteria such as a common topic of study or interest. A summary of types of grouping arrangements is shown in Figure 3.9. The purpose for each type of group is stated, sample activities are offered, and basic procedures are described.

TEXTBOOKS AND DIFFERENTIATED INSTRUCTION

Now more than ever before, learning to access, use, and evaluate information is a vital skill.

A textbook is a teaching tool. Although common in the past, the use of a single basal text is no longer sufficient for today's students. Now more than ever before, learning to access, use, and evaluate information is a vital skill. Confining students to a single text limits their perspective. Even at an early age, students must understand that information comes from a variety of sources. A textbook is one resource to use along with other print materials, Web sites, video documents, primary source documents, expert interviews, and so forth.

A criticism of American education is that it promotes superficial coverage of a vast amount of material with little opportunity for deep understanding to develop (Stigler & Hiebert, 1999). The volume of material contained in most textbooks and curriculum guides makes for a rushed and hurried coverage of content with little time to discuss and connect concepts. When teachers use the learning standards to sort out what is important for students to learn, they may find that not all the content contained in a textbook is necessary. They may also find that the textbook does not contain the material needed to meet the learning standards. Planning for differentiated instruction involves analyzing the materials available for learning and making choices as to what is necessary and what is not.

Beginning teachers usually feel more comfortable having the structure of a textbook to lean on. A textbook may provide resource information from which to obtain ideas on teaching strategies and student activities. Even beginning teachers, however, should use a variety of information sources in their planning and teaching.

PLANNING FOR SUCCESS IN DIFFERENTIATED INSTRUCTION

Differentiating instruction within a heterogeneous classroom requires precise planning, skillful execution, and detailed follow-up. It is a challenge to accommodate diverse student needs and maintain a realistic, manageable plan of instruction. Good and Brophy (1997) state that the effectiveness of a differentiated instructional approach is directly related to the teacher's managerial skills. An organized instructional plan is the first step to creating a productive, stimulating classroom environment.

Types of Grouping Arrangements

Grouping Arrangement	Purpose	Activities	Procedures
Whole Class	Introduce new academic concepts. Build social concept of community of learners.	• Introduce a concept. • Present information. • Outline directions. • Presentations and reports from cooperative groups. • Individual student reports.	Provide clear directions and purpose for the activity.
Partnering	Extend concepts and skills of two students as they work on a common task.	• Read aloud to build fluency. • Practice spelling words. • Reinforce vocabulary (unfamiliar words). • Reinforce word recognition. • Extend background information through graphic organizers. • Share written essays and stories. • Answer questions related to reading assignment (any content area). • Correct homework assignments.	Pair students based on ability levels, personalities, learning styles, interests, or any other characteristic that fits the purpose of the task. Build independence in partnering: model, practice, do, assess.
Cooperative Learning (Traditional and Modified)	Extend academic standards, social skills, positive relationships, and self-esteem through small-group participation.	• Research to answer content area questions. • Create mind maps to build background information and vocabulary. • Solve problems to build thinking skills.	• Form heterogeneous groups. • Assign (or select) roles. • Develop learning plan. • Build participation skills and social skills.

Figure 3.9   Types of Grouping Arrangements

Grouping Arrangement	Purpose	Activities	Procedures
Student-Led Discussion	Develop leadership and group participation skills through discussion of a common reading assignment.	• Guided reading follow-up discussion. • Independent reading follow-up discussion. Developing and responding to questions (literal and inferential).	Stages: 1. Teacher: directed (model and explain) 2. Transition (support and coach) 3. Student-led (observe)
Individual Projects and Assignments	Provide opportunities for students to work individually on development of concepts, skills, processes, and/or products.	Extend reading • Develop content knowledge. • Build background information. • Complete assignments.	Provide clear, specific directions and accountability measures.
Learning Centers	Provide a special work area where students engage in activities to reinforce concepts and skills.	Basic types of centers may focus on any content area: • Reading • Writing • Listening • Recording • Tech • Art • Music	Decide on setup options: 1. Assigned task, self-selected task, or exploration. 2. Timed or untimed 3. Assessed or "checked" Introduce the center. Provide clear and specific instructions for use-model, practice, do, assess.

Figure 3.9 (Continued)

Differentiated Assignments

Teachers who have not previously worked with differentiated groups should begin with small steps. The simplest way to start is by differentiating assignments that students complete while the teacher observes and monitors the process. Four differentiated assignment options ranging from simple to more complex are shown in Figure 3.10. Option one begins with individual work, option two incorporates partner activities, option three includes learning centers, and option four includes individual, partner, and learning center activities.

In the first option, there are two groups of students. The teacher has determined that 25 students need additional practice on a particular skill and 5 students have mastered the skill and are ready for extensional types

Differentiated Assignments in Class	
1	2 groups (5/25) • Students work independently on differentiated tasks • Teacher supervises students
2	2 groups (9/10) + 3 sets of 2 for partner work • Students work independently or with a partner on differentiated tasks • Teacher supervises students
3	15 students independent work + 2 learning centers (5 students each) • Students work independently or at a learning station • Teacher supervises students
4	9 students independent work + 2 learning centers (5 students each) + sets of 2 partner work • Students work independently, at a learning station, or with a partner • Teacher supervises students

Figure 3.10   Differentiated Assignments in Class

of activities. Activities and directions for completion are prepared as part of the planning process. In this option, even though students are working on the same activities, they are doing so individually. The teacher monitors students and offers assistance as needed. This option acquaints students with the idea that not everyone in the class does the same thing at the same time.

Option two shows two groups of students (a group of 9 and a group of 10). Each group works on a different assignment, but they do so as individuals, not groups. This option also shows 6 students who work on a partner activity. The role of the teacher is to monitor and observe students as they work.

Option three shows 15 students who work individually while 10 others work at learning centers. There are two learning centers with 5 students at each center.

Option four is the most ambitious with individual, partner, and learning center activities occurring simultaneously. It should be noted that this option is provided to show the range of activities possible; it is not meant as the best or most effective option.

Differentiation is not evaluated according to the number of groups or the complexity of group structures but rather on its efficiency and effectiveness in meeting students' needs. The purpose of differentiated assignments is to give students the practice, reinforcement, or extension they actually need. The role of the teacher using these options is to observe, assist, and coach students as they work independently. When students have demonstrated they can work independently, other differentiated learning options may be used.

Teacher-Directed Groups + Student Independent Groups	
1	• 1 teacher-directed group (15) • 1 independent-individual group (10)
2	• 1 teacher-directed group (19) • 3 sets partners (6)
3	• 1 teacher-directed group (8) • 3 sets partners (6) • 1 independent-individual work group (9)
4	• 1 teacher-directed group (5) • 3 sets partners (6) • 1 learning center (5) • 1 independent-individual work group (9)

Figure 3.11   Teacher-Directed Groups + Student Independent Groups

After students have been taught to work independently, with a partner, or in a small group, the teacher may begin working with small instructional groups such as guided reading groups. In guided reading, the teacher works with a small group of students at approximately the same reading level while the remaining students work independently.

Teacher-Directed Groups + Student Independent Groups

A collection of grouping plans that includes a teacher-directed group is shown in Differentiated Instruction: Teacher Directed Groups + Student Independent Groups (Figure 3.11). Plan 1 is a two-group option: the teacher instructs a group of 15 while 10 students work on individual tasks. Plan 2 shows a teacher-directed group of 19 while 6 students work as partners. Plan 3 shows a teacher-directed group of 8 students, three sets of partners, and a group of 9 students who work on individual activities. And Plan 4 adds a learning center for 5 students while three sets of partners work together, 9 students work on individual assignments, and the teacher instructs a group of 5 students. Getting students to work well as a group, independent of teacher supervision, requires planning and practicing. How students learn is just as important as what they learn.

Whole Class + Small Group + Individual Differentiation

Differentiation does not mean that students work on different activities all the time. There are times when whole-class instruction is the best teaching option. Students may be brought together as a whole class for an introductory lesson, overview, or directions. The following day individual or small-group activities are assigned as needed and continue as long as necessary. A concluding activity brings all students together again for reporting and sharing their completed assignments. An example of this type of differentiated schedule is shown in Figure 3.12. On Day 1, the teacher introduces the topic and explains the activities students are to complete. Days 2 and 3 involve small-group work; each group is assigned reading materials at their independent level. On Day 4, students work in pairs to edit and revise their written assignment. During this time, the teacher monitors and supervises students. On Day 5, students convene as a whole class to share their work. The amount of time allocated to

Whole-Class and Individual Differentiation

Major Topic:

Learning Standard(s):

	Day 1	Day 2	Day 3	Day 4	Day 5/6/7
Whole Class	• Preview topic • Provide directions for follow-up reading/writing assignments and report presentation				Report/present independent activities
Partner Work				• Peer Editing • Revising	
Group 1		Independent Reading: Text/Pages:	Independent Writing		
Group 2		Independent Reading: Text/Pages:	Independent Writing		
Group 3		Independent Reading: Text/Pages:	Independent Writing		

Figure 3.12   Whole-Class and Individual Differentiation

student reports is considered in terms of how many students will report and the length of each report. Certainly not all students need to present a report for each unit of instruction.

DESIGNING LEARNING ACTIVITIES TO DIFFERENTIATE INSTRUCTION

Learning activities must be aligned to the learning standards. Some learning standards require the student to know certain information or facts. Other learning standards require students to extend, perform, or apply their learning. The wording of the activity focuses and directs students to use certain types of thinking: literal, relational, transformational, and extensional. *Literal* activities are used to acquire basic information. *Relational* activities are used to connect information from various sources, including personal background knowledge. *Transformational* activities are used to manipulate, transcribe, or apply learning in a different way. And *extensional* activities are used to create, originate, evaluate, and in other ways produce something new. (See Designing Learning Activities, Figure 1.7, for commonly used terms in planning literal, relational, transformational, and extensional learning activities.) All students, regardless of instructional level, need opportunities to engage in all types of thinking. A differentiated activities matrix is a tool to assist the teacher in developing differentiated activities for students based on types of thinking. Differentiated activities shown on a differentiated activities matrix may be either content general or content specific. A content-general design is applicable for lessons of a common nature such as understanding literature, while a content-specific design is for a specific lesson or unit such as the Civil War.

Content-General Design

A content-general design contains activities that may apply to more than one lesson or unit. Since the activities are stated in general terms, it is possible to use them in more than one learning situation. The Differentiated Activities Matrix for Literature (Figure 3.13) is an example of a content-general differentiated plan for fiction reading at any grade level. The content-general matrix activities may be used to guide a group discussion or form the basis for written activities. These uses are discussed below.

Matrix as a Discussion Guide

During a discussion of a story or novel, the teacher may pose questions such as those in Figure 3.13 to elicit thinking from the literal/concrete to the extensional/abstract. Even in a heterogeneous classroom, all students may be drawn into the discussion through well-structured and strategically asked questions. The astute teacher builds students' confidence with easier questions and gradually challenges students to higher levels of thinking.

Differentiated Activities Matrix—Literature

Standard: Know the basic story elements as they relate to narrative fiction.

	Character(s)	Setting	Events	Problem	Solution
Literal	*Tell* about the main character, telling how he/she looks and acts.	*Identify* where the story takes place.	*Outline* the events in the story.	*Recall* and tell about the main problem in this story.	*Tell* about the solution to the problem in this story.
Relational	*Contrast* the main character in the story to someone you know.	*Compare* another place that is similar to the setting in this story.	*Describe* another story that had similar events.	*Explain* a similar problem in another story or in real life.	*Report* on an interview with one of the characters to find out their reaction to the solution.
Transformational	Select one of the characters and *tell* why that character is the most likable, bravest, least likable, most troublesome, etc.	*Change* this setting to where you live and tell how the story events would change.	a. *Dramatize* the events in the story. b. *Change* one event and tell how this would change the rest of the story.	Analyze the causes of the problem.	Select another possible solution to the problem and *rewrite* the story.
Extensional	a. *Develop* a new adventure to the story involving the same characters. b. *Develop* five questions that you would ask one of the characters in order to understand his or her actions.	a. *Design* a travel brochure telling about the location of the story. b. *Decide* whether or not you would like to live in this setting and give reasons for your response.	What was the most important event in this story? Give reasons for your response. (evaluation)	Assess how this problem might impact people other than the characters in the story.	*Develop an argument* to support the actions of the main character in resolving the problem in the story.

Figure 3.13 Differentiated Activities Matrix—Literature

Matrix as a Written Activities Plan

Any one of the differentiated activities presented in the Differentiated Activities Matrix for Literature (Figure 3.13) may be used as an individual or collaborative group project to be completed as a written activity. The teacher may assign the activity or students may be directed to self-select and complete one or more of the given activities.

Content-Specific Design

An example of a differentiated instructional design for specific content appears in the Differentiated Activities Matrix for the U.S. Civil War (Figure 3.14). In this example, the more general learning standards related to the key events, factors, and impact of the American Civil War are itemized into more specific learning standards related to causes, battles, commerce, international relations, and outcomes. The student activities for each of the specific learning standards range from literal (i.e., listing the major causes leading to the Civil War) to extensional (i.e., developing an argument to support the actions of President Lincoln in bringing the war to an end).

Another example, Differentiated Activities Matrix for Health, is shown in Figure 3.15. The learning standards shown here are general statements that must be specified further in order to be useful in planning instruction (Skowron, 2000). In this case, the learning standards are specified as the respiratory system organs, functions, illnesses, and well-being.

As with the content-general design, a content-specific design may be used for individual or collaborative-group activities. The teacher may assign the activities, or students may select the activities they will complete.

PLANNING DIFFERENTIATED INSTRUCTION

Differentiated instruction includes the same components as basic lesson planning; however, there are multiple lessons planned to accommodate students' needs. Differentiated instruction also may include many of the elements of integrated instruction as two or more learning standards or performance descriptors are combined in one lesson. Differentiated instruction involves many components that must be carefully orchestrated to avoid curriculum gaps and confusion.

Develop the Rationale for Differentiated Instruction

The first question to answer when planning to differentiate instruction is, "Why is there a need to differentiate instruction?" Valid reasons should exist for differentiation of activities. Differentiation may not always be a desirable option. When students have similar needs, differentiation may not be necessary. When students' diversity contributes to the learning of others, whole-class activities may be preferable. Understanding the characteristics of the students in the class helps to form the rationale for using a differentiated instructional design.

Differentiated Activities Matrix: American History

Learning Standard: Know the key events, factors, and impact of the American Civil War.

Specific content → / Type of activity ↓	Know the major causes leading to the Civil War.	Know the major battles of the Civil War.	Know the impact of the Civil War on commerce.	Know about U.S. international relations during the Civil War.	Know the factors that brought the Civil War to an end.
Literal	*List* the major causes leading to the Civil War.	*Tell* the major battles fought during the Civil War.	*Identify* three major trade and commerce difficulties during the Civil War.	*Name* the other countries involved in the American Civil War.	*Tell* about three major outcomes of the Civil War.
Relational	*Explain* the causes of the Civil War from the North's (South's) point of view.	a. *Describe* one Civil War battle including preparation, setting, people, events, and outcome. b. *Compare* one battle won by the North with another won by the South. Tell why it was won and what happened as a result.	*Summarize* the reasons for problems with trade during the Civil War.	*Discuss* how other nations responded to the American Civil War.	Conduct a hypothetical interview with a southern plantation owner (slave, 10-year-old boy, businessman, entertainer, etc.) and *interpret* his or her views on the outcome of the war.
Transformational	*Change or add* a historical event and tell how this might have changed the North's (or South's) decision to go to war.	*Dramatize* a trial for one of the northern generals captured by the South.	Would trade and commerce problems be *similar* in other wars? Give reasons for your response.	Were the causes of the American Civil War *similar* to civil wars in other countries?	Could there have been solutions to the problems faced by the North and South other than war? (*analysis*)
Extensional	a. *Develop* five questions you would ask President Lincoln regarding his decision to go to war. (A classroom partner will answer the questions.) b. *Prove* that these historical events (causes) justify war.	*Draw or depict* a specific Civil War battlefield showing location, troops, artillery, camps, civilian presence.	a. *Design* a plan for a Northern manufacturer of shoes to sell his goods in the South before and during the war. b. *Justify or prove* why it was legal (or illegal) for northern manufacturers to sell their goods to the South.	a. *Create* a map showing international involvement in the Civil War. b. Was French support for the South justified? Give reasons (*proof*) for your answer.	a. *Create* a timeline showing the major events of the war and a map of the country after northern victory. b. Develop an *argument* to support the actions of President Lincoln in bringing the war to an end.

Figure 3.14 Differentiated Activities Matrix: American History

87

Differentiated Activities Matrix for Health

Health Learning Standards:

1. Describe and explain the structure and functions of the human body's systems and how they interrelate.

2. Apply decision-making skills related to the promotion and protection of individual health.

3. Explain the basic principles of health promotion, illness prevention, and safety.

Content: The Respiratory System: Organs, Functions, Illnesses, and Well-Being

	Organs	**Functions**	**Illnesses**	**Well-Being**
Literal	*List* the organs in the human respiratory system.	*Tell* what each organ in the respiratory system does.	*List* the kinds of illnesses that involve the respiratory system.	*Outline* the section in your text on respiratory health.
Relational	*Explain* how the respiratory system influences other organs of the body.	*Compare* the human respiratory system to the respiratory system of a fish.	*Explain* how respiratory illnesses influence the rest of the body.	*Summarize* the important points for maintaining a healthy respiratory system.
Transformational	*Demonstrate* the human respiratory system using a bellows, balloon, tubing, and other materials.	*Research* the respiratory system of the gorilla and *contrast* it to the human respiratory system.	*Research* the causes of respiratory illnesses and *explain* how they can be avoided.	*Apply* the features and workings of a mechanical respirator to the human respiratory system.
Extensional	*Evaluate* the two sides of the organ donation debate.	What is the most important organ in the respiratory system? *Justify* your answer.	*Justify* why students should or should not stay home from school when they are sick.	*Develop* an argument against smoking.

Figure 3.15   Differentiated Activities Matrix for Health

Make the Commitment

It is certainly possible for a teacher to differentiate instruction within her or his own classroom, but it is worth the time and effort to plan differentiation as a whole-school effort. This provides consistency and continuity of philosophy and practices as students move through the grades. It also provides collegial support and a team effort that makes planning easier. A written statement developed by the staff affirming their commitment to meeting students' needs through differentiation communicates to parents and the community that each student is helped to develop to his or her fullest potential.

Plan the Desired Results: Standards and Performance Descriptors

Standards and performance descriptors are the basis for planning differentiated instruction. It is important for teachers to be thoroughly familiar with the standards as they plan instruction and to document that the standards are being taught. Students may be grouped for instruction based not only on instructional needs but also on how they best learn.

Plan Assessment: Evidence of Learning

Planning assessment in a differentiated classroom is essentially the same as planning assessment in other contexts. Assessment must align to the learning standards and performance descriptors and provide feedback to teacher and students on progress being made. In a differentiated classroom, assessment formats may differ for students based on how they were grouped (i.e., reading level, learning preferences, interests). The assessment format may be performance-based with rubrics for scoring, or the assessment format may be a pencil-and-paper, selected-response test. All assessments must be aligned to the learning standards and the instructional activities. Alignment helps to ensure that students are assessed on what they are taught.

Develop the Differentiated Instructional Design

A differentiated instructional design contains appropriate strategies and learning activities that are directly related to the learning standards. In a differentiated classroom, student groups are formed based on common instructional needs or other characteristics. This requires a separate plan for each group. To maintain a manageable plan, the number of groups formed should be somewhat limited. Too many groups will require too many activities, which may make management difficult. It is best to begin with a few activities and increase the number as both teacher and students become comfortable and experienced with this instructional approach.

A differentiated instructional design plan documents and communicates to others what learning standards are being addressed in the classroom. It may be a simple design based on a few learning standards and activities or a more complex design incorporating several standards integrated across content areas. However, the design should never become so complex as to be overwhelming to the students or the teacher. Beginning with a simple design and expanding over the years is an efficient and manageable way to plan.

Construct the Instructional Activities Matrix

A differentiated instructional design matrix (Figures 3.13, 3.14, and 3.15) is a framework that organizes and documents instructional activities. The column heads list the learning standards; the row heads list the basis for differentiation. For example, if differentiation is to occur based on types of thinking, the types of thinking are listed as row heads. If differentiation is to occur based on Gardner's eight intelligences, the intelligences become the row heads. A specific, well-planned design makes implementation manageable and efficient.

The matrix is a planning tool that allows flexibility in what is to be differentiated and the types of activities to develop. Standards and performance descriptors drive the planning process and are always listed as column heads.

Instructional Activities and Grouping Arrangements

Standard: Know and apply concepts that describe how living things interact with each other and with their environment.

Content: Understand the relationships of living things to the Arctic environment.

Grouping Arrangement: I = Individual activity; **P** = Partner activity; **SG** = Small-group activity; **TW** = Teacher-directed activity—whole class; **TSG** = Teacher-directed activity—small group

	Weather, Climate and Geography	Life Forms	Global Importance
Literal	Draw a picture of the Artic landscape including the features discussed in class. (**I**)	List the animals that live in the Arctic. Tell about one that is most interesting to you. (**I**)	
Relational	Compare the weather of the Arctic to our winter weather. (**TSG & I**)	Compare the fish that live in the Arctic with the fish found in Lake Michigan. (**TSG**)	Discuss the importance of the Arctic in terms of global well-being. (**TW**) Discuss the impact of our dependence on oil on the Arctic environment. (**TW**)
Transfor-mational		Think what it must be like for people to live in the Arctic. Tell what a day would be like for someone your age. (**P**) How do polar bears (or any other animal) depend on their environment for life? (**I**)	
Extensional		Create a "new" animal that could live in the Arctic. Describe the animal: how it looks, what it eats, and where it lives. (**P**)	Write a letter to the president of Standard Oil telling why the Arctic is important to you and your family. (**I**)

Figure 3.16   Instructional Activities and Grouping Arrangements

Coordinate Instructional Activities and Grouping Arrangements

A differentiated instruction matrix lists activities in relation to types of thinking and the key elements contained in the learning standards. Teachers also may use the matrix to coordinate student grouping arrangements to help ensure that all students have the opportunity to be involved at all levels of thinking. Activities may be done individually, with a partner, in a small-group setting, in a whole-class setting, or as a teacher-directed small group. An example of a coordinated plan is shown in Figure 3.16. Keep in mind that the matrix need not contain an activity in each cell. The activities that are included should be interesting, purposeful, and worthy of the student's time. There should be a balance among the types of activities, and students should have opportunities to engage in all types of cognitive tasks. Rubrics that clearly convey the criteria and expectations for performance should be used whenever appropriate.

Develop Specific Lesson Plans

The alignment of standards, assessment, and instructional activities is the foundation for the lesson plan. Figure 3.17 is an example of a specific lesson plan that includes some of the activities contained in the Instructional Activities and Grouping Arrangements matrix (Figure 3.16).

USING THE DIFFERENTIATED INSTRUCTIONAL DESIGN PLANNING GUIDE

The Differentiated Instructional Design Planning Guide (Figure 3.18) is a tool to assist teachers in thinking through all the components of planning differentiated instruction. It comprises three sections: Section 1: Desired Results—Standards and Performance Descriptors; Section 2: Assessment—Evidence of Learning; and Section 3: Lesson Design. Each of these three sections includes three columns: "Planning Questions and Decisions," "Information and Data Sources," and "Notes and Comments." The Planning Questions and Decisions column poses a series of key questions to guide and stimulate thinking during the planning process. The Information and Data Sources column lists the types of resources and data sources that will facilitate answering the questions in column one. The Notes and Comments column provides information that will further clarify and assist in answering the questions in column one. An example of how an eighth grade language arts teacher used the planning guide is shown in Figure 3.19.

Teachers who have little or no previous experience in planning differentiated instruction will find the planning guide a supportive scaffold in their initial efforts. Novice and preservice teachers will find it helpful to follow all the steps in the planning guide. As a result, subsequent planning will be easier. Experienced teachers with an understanding of differentiated instructional design may find that they need only review the planning guide and focus on those areas that will enhance their planning efforts. This guide is a helpful planning tool, but experienced teachers know that change options and flexibility for improvisation as the plan unfolds are also possible. Planning differentiated instruction involves the following steps:

1. Read the planning guide in its entirety.

It is good practice to become thoroughly familiar with the planning guide before using it. This will save time in the long run. Get the big picture in mind before filling in the details.

Lesson Plan

<u>Learning Standards</u> **(concepts, skills, processes)**

Understand the relationships of living things to the Arctic environment.

<u>Lesson Design</u>	<u>Materials</u>	**<u>Student Grouping</u>**
• **Opening (outcomes/purpose/expectations)** Picture of Arctic covered with paper. Use hints and clues and predictions to determine what the picture is.	Picture of Arctic landscape	Whole group
• **Teaching Strategies/Activities (demonstration, modeling, explanation, directions, etc.)** 1. Discuss geography, climate of Arctic. 2. Introduce and distribute student books: • *Awesome Arctic* (Group 1) • *Near the North Pole* (Group 2) • *Arctic Adventure* (Group 3) 3. Give directions: Read assigned pages in your book. Choose an individual activity to work on. Be sure to review the rubric for your activity before you begin.	Globe Maps Pictures Student-leveled books Activity file and rubrics	Whole group
• **Student Activities** (See sample instructional activities matrices)		Individual
• **Closing (connections/summary/reflection)** Discussion of key points, what was learned.		Whole class
<u>Practice Activities/Assignments</u> Complete any unfinished work as homework.		
<u>Assessment of Student Learning</u> Observation during discussion.		Whole class

Date: Time:

Notes/Comments:

Figure 3.17   Lesson Plan

2. Think through each section of the planning guide.

Begin with Section 1: Desired Results—Standards and Performance Descriptors. Think about the questions in column one and write down your thoughts and ideas. Consult the data and information sources suggested in column two and note the reminders and supplemental information in column three. Add notes and comments of your own that will be helpful in subsequent planning. Planning questions may be deleted or added to fit your situation.

Continue through Section 2: Assessment—Evidence of Learning and Section 3: Lesson Design.

3. Synthesize information.

The thinking process described above provides a great deal of information which now must be synthesized into a coherent plan. First determine the basis for differentiation: reading levels, types of thinking, learning styles, interests. Plan the differentiated activities based on the standards and performance descriptors. Use of a differentiated instruction matrix to document activities is helpful but optional. It may be more efficient to develop lesson plans for each group.

SUMMARY OF GENERAL PLANNING STEPS FOR DIFFERENTIATED INSTRUCTION

The Differentiated Instructional Design Planning Guide (Figure 3.18) contains the detailed description of what must be considered in planning differentiated instruction. This is the foundation for developing specific instructional plans. The steps below are a general outline of the process:

1. Think through the process of differentiated instruction using the Differentiated Instructional Design Planning Guide (Figure 3.18, and the reproducible, pp. 102–103).

2. Determine the rationale for using a differentiated instructional approach.

3. Determine categories for differentiation.

4. Determine what learning standards will be addressed.

5. Decide how specific elements of the learning standard will be assessed.

6. Develop activities based on category for differentiation and learning standard. Use the differentiated activities matrix reproducible (p. 104) to plan instructional activities.

7. Develop specific lessons as needed to show organization and timing.

The associated planning and teaching techniques incorporated in differentiated instructional design evolve as teachers become experienced and comfortable with this approach. Teachers who use differentiated instruction generally begin by implementing short units, which are modified and expanded over time. Planning differentiated instruction coordinates student learning characteristics (how students learn) with learning standards (what students learn). Darling-Hammond (1997) states, "There is no prepackaged set of steps or lessons that will secure understanding for every learner in the same way" (p. 74). Research supports teaching practices that honor the individuality of students in terms of their experiences, interests, and prior knowledge.

DIFFERENTIATED INSTRUCTIONAL DESIGN PLANNING GUIDE

SECTION 1: Desired Results—Standards and Performance Descriptors

Differentiated instruction is grounded on the standards and performance descriptors. Use these questions to plan a differentiated instructional design.

Planning Questions and Decisions	Information and Data Sources	Notes and Comments
1. Why is there a need to differentiate instruction?	Review student data, performance, observations, and professional literature.	The decision and subsequent planning for differentiated instruction may be before a unit of study or any time during a unit of study when it becomes apparent that differentiation is needed to accommodate students' needs.
2. How will students be grouped for differentiation (levels of performance, interests, learning styles)?	Student data on performance levels, interests, or learning styles may be used to determine instructional activity groups.	An informal student interest survey, observational checklist, or pretest may supply additional data.
3. What are the learning standards to be taught?	Review content, skills, process, and concept standards required at district and state level.	Select those standards that will be made more meaningful through differentiation.
4. How will learning standards be organized and documented?	A differentiated instructional design matrix may be used to plan and keep track of differentiated activities.	Once the learning standards and the basis for differentiation are decided, a differentiated instructional matrix is developed. Specific activities will be added later. The matrix documents the standards, activities, and categories of differentiation.

Figure 3.18   Differentiated Instructional Design Planning Guide

SECTION 2: Assessment—Evidence of Learning

Assessment of students must be aligned to what students should know and be able to do as defined in the learning standards and performance descriptors. Use these questions as a thinking guide to plan assessment procedures.

Planning Questions and Decisions	Information and Data Sources	Notes and Comments
1. How will student learning be assessed?	Refer to curriculum resource information and best practices information related to types of assessment.	Planning for assessment is a recursive process. Assessment strategies and tools are tentatively outlined in the initial stages of instructional design, reconsidered and modified as the design emerges, and then finalized with the final product. Students are held responsible for the learning inherent in the activities they have performed.
2. What assessment materials are available and what materials need to be developed? Are combined or embedded assessments feasible?	Review: a. Required and optional assessments b. Rubrics and assessments in district curriculum guides, teacher manuals, other sources	
3. How will the assessment be scored?		Design appropriate rubrics to show criteria and expectations for performance. Consider student participation in design of rubrics. A differentiated classroom may have common assessments; however, students should be held responsible only for what they have been taught.
4. How will learning be reported?	Check schoolwide or districtwide requirements and policies related to grading.	If a schoolwide grading scale is required, be sure to align rubric levels with the grading scale. Consider the development and use of student portfolios as a means of providing feedback to students and parents.
5. What further practice and follow-up assessment can be provided for students who fall below expectations?	Review available commercially prepared assessments.	It is efficient to have a file of alternative practice activities and test forms available when needed. Consider creating or selecting these as the lesson is developed.
6. How will the assessment results be used?	Review district policies and handbooks that describe the use of assessment results.	Use assessment results to determine student strengths and weaknesses and plan the next lessons.

Figure 3.18 (Continued)

SECTION 3: Lesson Design

Differentiated instruction involves many components and different lessons for different learners. Consider these questions as a thinking guide as you plan differentiated lessons.

Planning Questions and Decisions	Information and Data Sources	Notes and Comments
1. What are the specific learning standards/benchmarks to be taught?	Refer to the Differentiated Instructional Design Planning Guide—Section 1.	Alignment of standards, assessment, and instruction is imperative.
2. What are the categories of differentiation?	Analyze student assessment results to group students based on achievement levels. Other sources of information include student profiles and interest inventories.	Students should participate as members of many groups. Do not limit differentiation to achievement levels only.
3. What activities correlate to each standard and each differentiation category?	Curriculum guides, teaching manuals, professional literature, best practices information, etc., are sources of information for ideas and activities. Use the Differentiated Instructional Design Planning Matrix to document the standards and activities.	In some cases, activities may overlap to such a degree that they are not really different. When this is the case, leave that box on the matrix planning chart blank. It is not necessary to fill in an activity for every box on the matrix.
4. How long will this instructional unit last? How long will each activity take?	Calendar of school events, holidays, curriculum pacing guides, and testing schedules are sources of information for scheduling.	Develop a specific organized calendar and schedule for the activities. Balance the amount of time with the priority or importance of the activity.
5. How will the lessons and activities be organized?	Refer to the Basic Instructional Design Planning Guide described in Chapter 1 (Figure 1.10).	Even when most standards are taught through differentiated activities, there may be times when it is appropriate to conduct lessons on common needs with the entire class or with a small group. Each lesson will contain all the components of the basic lesson design: • Motivating opening • Teaching/learning strategies • Materials and resources • Grouping • Closure • Follow-up practice • Assessment
6. Are there any foreseeable pitfalls in this lesson?		Think ahead to avoid potential difficulties.
7. What will I do if the lesson/unit doesn't work out?		A "fallback" plan can keep a "flop" from becoming a "disaster."

Figure 3.18 (Continued)

DIFFERENTIATED INSTRUCTIONAL DESIGN: EXAMPLE FROM GRADE 8 LANGUAGE ARTS

SECTION 1: Desired Results—Standards and Performance Descriptors

Example: Grade 8 Language Arts Class

Planning Questions and Decisions

1. Why is there a need to differentiate instruction?

My students exhibit a wide range of reading abilities. I would like to find some way to meet their needs yet still have them participate as a whole group. I have tried in-class ability grouping using different textbooks and was not pleased with it. Students were too segregated. I would like to give them reading assignments on the same general topic but allow them to read material at their level. I could then have them discuss books around a common theme.

2. How will students be grouped for differentiation (levels of performance, interests, learning styles)?

Last year's test results show a wide range of reading abilities. Students will be grouped based on a reading level range. Within each range activities will be selected to tap into more transformational and extensional activities.

3. What are the learning standards to be taught?

Learning objectives relate to the basic story elements: character, setting, events, problem, solution. I would also like students to make connections to previous readings or information they have related to the story. Activities will be group discussion and one individual writing assignment.

4. How will learning standards be organized and documented?

The Differentiated Activities Matrix will be used to document the various activities for each group based on the story elements.

Figure 3.19   Differentiated Instructional Design: Example From Grade 8 Language Arts

SECTION 2: Assessment—Evidence of Learning

Example: Grade 8 Language Arts Class

	1. How will students demonstrate their learning?	2. How will the assessment be scored?	3. How will the assessment be reported?	4. How will the assessment results be used?
Assessment 1	All students will complete a story map graphic organizer describing the story components.	Story maps will be assessed with a rubric.	Students will receive a copy of the story map rubric scoring results. They will have the opportunity to add to the story map if there are any noted deficiencies.	Assessment results will provide feedback for the students and the teacher regarding comprehension of the story. Scores will be included in the student's quarterly grade report for language arts.
Assessment 2	Students will self-select 3 activities to complete from the Differentiated Activities Matrix. Each selected activity must be from a different row.	The students' written responses will not be scored but will be used in a compare/contrast group discussion of the books.	Students will be assessed on the degree of participation in discussion—none, limited, and involved.	The degree of participation will provide feedback for the student and the teacher on how ideas are communicated.
Assessment 3	One of the self-selected activities will be submitted as a written assignment.	Written assignments will be assessed with the appropriate rubric—narrative, descriptive/ expository, or persuasive. Students will determine which rubric is to be used according to what type of writing they did.	Copy of the rubric will be returned to the student with teacher's scoring and comments. Students will be asked to use the rubric to self-score their writing.	Copies of the teacher's scores and the student's scores will be sent home to parents. The teacher's scores will be included in the student's quarterly grade report for language arts.

Figure 3.19 (Continued)

SECTION 3: Lesson Design

Example: Grade 8 Language Arts Class

1. What are the specific learning standards to be taught?

The learning standards relate to the basic story components: characters, setting, problem, events, and solution. The Differentiated Instruction Matrix documents the learning standards and how they will be met based on students' reading levels.

2. What are the categories of differentiation?

There are three categories for differentiation: grade level reading ability, above grade level reading ability, and below grade level reading ability. Students will be grouped according to my observations and test scores. If this goes well, I may try to extend the categories based on books that are selected by the students.

3. What activities correlate to each objective and each differentiation category?

Activities will be written out using the terms that correspond to literal, relational, transformational, and extensional learning. Activities will be documented on the Differentiated Instruction Matrix.

4. How long will the activities take?

It is expected that students will do the reading in class and at home and then complete the activities in class over a period of eight school days. Since this is a "first run." the time period may be adjusted to be more or less than eight days. Group three will need more time since I will work with them initially.

5. How will the lessons and activities be organized?

I plan to use the standard lesson plan format. I'll work out the time to do a vocabulary introduction activity and a DRTA for the first chapter with group three. This will provide some support and hopefully build confidence for reading the rest of the book on their own.

6. Are there any foreseeable pitfalls in this lesson?

I'll have to monitor students closely since this will be their first experience with group work.

7. What will I do if the lesson/unit doesn't work out?

I could eliminate the group work but it is more likely that I will work through any rough spots and adjust accordingly.

Figure 3.19 (Continued)

REFLECTIVE PRACTICE: INNER DIALOGUE

Merely following an outline or filling in a template is not sufficient to develop expertise in planning powerful lessons. Planning is a metacognitive, reflective process in which the teacher thinks, reflects, adjusts, redirects, fiddles, and fine-tunes the various components until a powerful lesson emerges. When reflection is an intrinsic part of the instructional planning process and teachers take time to analyze their planning efforts, they learn through their experiences, and future planning becomes more effective and efficient.

What Costa (1991) calls "inner dialogue" is essential to professional growth, change, and improvement. Use the Inner Dialogue page (Figure 3.20) to reflect on planning actions, attempts, and results of using the integrated instructional design. Be open-minded but skeptical. Consider pros and cons, benefits, and challenges. Look beyond what was accomplished to why and how it was accomplished.

Inner Dialogue

Reflect on the planning process to deepen your understanding. Keep your notes and refer to them when you plan again.

This is what I did in the planning process.	This is what I think about it and how I might change or modify it.
Some new learning	
Some benefits	
Some challenges	

Figure 3.20 Inner Dialogue

DIFFERENTIATED INSTRUCTIONAL DESIGN: PLANNING QUESTIONS AND DECISIONS

Desired Results	1. Why is there a need to differentiate instruction?
	2. How will students be grouped for differentiation (levels of performance, interests, learning styles)?
	3. What are the learning standards to be taught?
	4. How will learning standards be organized and documented?
Assessment: Evidence Learning	5. How will students demonstrate their learning?
	6. How will the assessment be scored?
	7. How will assessment results be communicated to students and parents?
	8. How will the assessment results be used?

Lesson Design	9. What are the specific learning standards/benchmarks to be taught?
	10. What are the categories of differentiation?
	11. What activities will be planned to align to the learning standards and the differentiation category?
	12. How long will the lesson/activities take?
	13. How will lessons and activities be organized?
	14. Are there any foreseeable pitfalls in this lesson?
	15. What will I do if the lesson/unit doesn't work out?

DIFFERENTIATED ACTIVITIES PLANNING MATRIX

A differentiated planning matrix is a planning tool for teachers to differentiate cognitive tasks (row headings) in relation to content area objectives (column headings).

Standard, Specific Elements Type of Learning							
Literal Learning							
Relational Learning							
Transformational Learning							
Extensional Learning							

INDIVIDUAL LEARNING ACTIVITY

Learning standard/performance descriptor:
Task description:
Special features:
Wing dings:
Timeline and date due:
Organization and storage:
Bonuses:

LEARNING CENTER PLAN

Center:

Purpose:

Location:

Activities:

Materials:

Preparation and directions:

Accountability measures:

PROJECT PACK

Name: _____   **Starting date:** _____

Timeline	Task	Date completed

Things to keep in your folder:	Materials in your Project Pack:

Problem-Based Learning Instructional Design

4

Problem-based learning has roots in the philosophy of Dewey (1913) and the theory of constructivism (Brooks & Brooks, 1993). According to Nagel (1999), problem-based learning is student centered, inquiry oriented, curriculum integrated, and collaborative. It begins with an "ill-structured" problem springboard in which students are given minimal guidelines and information to begin. They must discuss and specifically define the problem and then, using a process much like the scientific method, work through to a solution or conclusion. Problem-based learning is touted as being as "authentic as it gets" (Stepien & Gallagher, 1993).

Problem-based learning (PBL) was developed at the McMaster University School of Medicine in Canada during the 1960s by Dr. Howard Barrow. In the United States, several medical schools, including Harvard University's School of Medicine, adopted a PBL model as an alternative to the traditional lecture-dominated approach to learning. Problem-based learning is finding acceptance at other levels of education as well, as teachers become convinced of its effectiveness and acquire expertise in using it as an instructional strategy (Aspy, Aspy, & Quinby, 1993; Delisle, 1997).

Project-based learning is very similar in intent and design to problem-based learning. As presented here, the purposes and procedures for problem-based learning also apply to project-based learning. The Buck Institute for Education offers information and examples of project-based learning on their Web site (www.bie .org).

PROBLEM-BASED LEARNING EXAMINED

Problem-based learning is an approach that capitalizes on students' interest in real-life problems. It is a "process" approach rather than a "content" approach. Students acquire content information and knowledge by using processes such as exploration, research, and collaboration. Students learn to formulate a problem statement, develop action plans, conduct information searches, use data, find and use resources, work collaboratively with others both within the school and outside the school, arrive at conclusions, and communicate findings to others.

Problem-based learning is an approach that capitalizes on students' interest in real-life problems. It is a "process" approach rather than a "content" approach.

109

Even very young children may be involved in projects that engage them in questioning, hypothesizing, and predicting (Checkley, 1997; Helm, 2004). Exposure to the problem-based process at an early age helps students to develop the attitude that learning is the search for information to resolve problems.

Theories of constructivism support learning approaches that enable students to engage in activities in which they make sense of ideas and connect new information and concepts to what they already know. The theories of both John Dewey and Jean Piaget point to the importance of engagement in meaningful learning activities. John Dewey believed that students construct knowledge through experiences that are meaningful to them. He also believed that these experiences must occur in social situations in which students work together. Jean Piaget believed that discovery leads to constructing knowledge and is fundamental to learning at each stage of development (Brooks & Brooks, 1993).

Constructivist theory fits with brain-based theories that describe learning as connecting new information and concepts to what is already known (Caine & Caine, 1991; Jensen, 2000). New learning must be fitted into what is already established to be meaningful and lasting. Students who apply their learning in new situations are more likely to gain deeper understandings (McTigue, Seif, & Wiggins, 2004).

Problem-based learning activities that engage students in personal and interesting ways can increase motivation and desire to learn.

Problem-based learning activities that engage students in personal and interesting ways can increase motivation and the desire to learn. Classrooms can be dynamic places where students and teachers are energized about learning, but it takes more than just a problem to excite students. Teachers need to share their own passion for learning, know how to relate to students, and provide the setting and resources that allow students to pursue meaning (Intrator, 2004).

THE ROLE OF LEARNING STANDARDS IN A PROBLEM-BASED LEARNING CLASSROOM

Problem-based learning, by its very nature, integrates learning standards, but the standards involved in the PBL activity may not be completely known initially. As the problem unfolds and students work toward its solution, the associated learning standards may change. Effective planning for problem-based learning requires teachers to have in-depth knowledge of the learning standards—to recognize where they occur in the problem activity and ensure they are assessed in some manner. This is not to say that the teacher does no preliminary planning. In planning for problem-based learning, the teacher begins with some learning standards in mind but must be willing to add or delete standards as the problem unfolds and the activity is under way. This requires a highly organized, astute teacher who observes students as they plan and notes the important learning standards they will address in their study. The teacher must have a high level of ambiguity tolerance—the ability to work with a degree of vagueness and uncertainty. In addition, the teacher must be able to pull together resources in short order, plan lessons (sometimes on the spot), and constantly think ahead to where the students may lead. The Problem-Based Learning Standards Overview (Figure 4.1) may be used to document and keep track of the learning standards involved in the study of a particular problem. The standards overview form is a flexible document. It is adjusted as the teacher notes the changes in the direction students take in their problem solving.

Problem-Based Learning
Standards Overview Example

This overview shows the possible standards that may be embedded in a problem at the initial stages of discussion. The standards will be refined and modified throughout the problem-based project.

The Problem

Some students are complaining about the food in the school cafeteria. There is a general feeling that the food is tasteless and high in calories. Is this complaint well founded? How may it be remedied?

Reading Standards

1. Draw conclusions from printed information.
2. Demonstrate understanding of visual information.
3. Differentiate between fact and opinion.

Writing Standards

1. Develop a well-organized report.
2. Write letters of inquiry.

Listening/Speaking Standards

1.
2. NA
3.

Physical Education and Health Standards

1. Demonstrate understanding of the calorie/weight relationship.
2. Develop a healthy, tasty menu.

Science Standards

1.
2. NA
3.

Social Studies Standards (History, Geography, Economics, etc.)

1.
2. NA
3.

Fine Arts Standards

1.
2. NA
3.

Mathematics Standards

1. Collect data (survey, interviews, observations).
2. Draw conclusions from data.
3. Construct graphs and charts from data.

Figure 4.1   Problem-Based Learning Standards Overview

PLANNING FOR PROBLEM-BASED LEARNING

The First Step

Problem-based learning begins with an "ill-structured" problem that gives students just enough information to entice them to begin a discussion and make connections to previous learning. The Problem-Based Learning Initiative at Southern Illinois University describes a problem as a "goal where the correct path to its solution is not known" (www.pbli.org). The problem deals with some real-life issue of interest to the students. If the goal of education is to prepare students to solve real-life problems, then ill-structured problems are the most authentic (Checkley, 1997). In real life, rarely is all necessary information readily apparent when one encounters a problem. And rarely does a real-life problem have only one right solution. It is the task of the students to examine and further define the problem and construct a hypothesis statement. Topics for problem-based learning activities come from real-life issues and problems (Figure 4.2).

Delisle (1997) says that an ill-structured problem should be developmentally appropriate, grounded in student experience, and curriculum based and should allow for a variety of teaching and learning strategies and styles.

According to Stepien, Gallagher, and Workman (1993),

1. Students will need more information than what is initially presented. This helps them to understand more fully what is needed for a solution.

2. There are no right or wrong ways to study a problem. The process depends on the problem itself and the questions generated as the focus for the study.

3. The problem itself may change as information is collected.

4. There are no right or wrong solutions.

Next Steps

When the problem is defined, students plan a course of action and determine how they will go about reaching a solution. Their actions may involve study, research, interviews, and data collection using a variety of resources. Students hone their reasoning and logical thinking through participating in realistic and relevant problem-solving activities. The process is iterative in that as new information is acquired, the problem statement may be altered and the course of action changed (Checkley, 1997). During this stage, the teacher facilitates student discussion and actions. Traditional lesson plans do not fit problem-based lessons; however, the teacher should keep a record of information related to what students do as they pursue the solution to the problem. Students may also be asked to keep a journal or log of their daily activities.

In a problem-based learning setting, students explore beyond the walls of the classroom to collect data that contribute to the solution of the problem. The problem itself is most often related to issues and events of the larger

Topics for Problem-Based Learning Units

Wildlife in Suburbia

Some people are complaining about deer destroying plants and foliage on their property. The Animal Control Agency feels it is important for everyone to understand the reasons why deer are here and what can be done to coexist.

Nutrition Is Important

Do healthy eating habits build strong bones, bodies, and minds? Develop a poster campaign to teach others the necessity of eating nutritious foods.

The Invisible World

We can't see them, but we often feel their power. Germs and bacteria can make us sick. How can we convince students to wash their hands and use good hygiene habits?

Unpredictable Weather

Weather forecasts sometimes run awry. Rain showers, lower temperatures, and even severe weather can happen unexpectedly. Why is it difficult to forecast the weather accurately? How can we explain the difficulty to others?

Building Boom

Vacant land and farmland is fast disappearing. Homes and shopping malls now stand where corn and wheat once grew. What impact will building development have on the environment?

Safety Is Everyone's Concern

Every year children are hurt or killed crossing railroad tracks. How can we help educate young children about the dangers of railroad crossings?

Playground Design

The PTA has donated funds to construct a playground behind the school. What type of play equipment should be installed? Where should it be placed? How can the playground be made safe as well as inviting to children?

Technology and Learning

Computers help us learn in many ways. How can we explain to our parents and grandparents how we use computers and what we learn from them?

Pit Bull Controversy

Pit bull dogs have received much media attention lately due to their attacks on children and adults. What's behind these attacks? Are pit bulls vicious dogs that should not be allowed as pets? Or are they misunderstood or mistreated creatures? Develop an argument for your point of view based on researched evidence.

Figure 4.2   Topics for Problem-Based Learning Units

community. The process of learning through problem solving involves coming to terms with what is known or believed and fitting this with new information. New information may conflict with existing perspectives, ideas, and attitudes. Reconciling the new and the old becomes part of the learning process.

EFFECTIVELY LEADING PROBLEM-BASED LEARNING

Problem-based learning is student centered. Students take the lead in planning, directing, and completing their work. They choose resources and evaluate their progress. Effective problem-based learning incorporates many teaching and learning strategies.

The Teacher's Role in Problem-Based Learning

In problem-based learning, the teacher allows the students to take the lead. The predominant role of the teacher is that of facilitator and coach who provides resources, asks questions to guide students, and helps them to understand their own thinking as they work through the problem. There is a great deal of ambiguity involved in problem-based learning, and teachers must be knowledgeable and confident in the methodology to be successful (Checkley, 1997). The teacher must be an astute observer and listener to understand students' needs and offer assistance, resources, or instruction at the appropriate time. The teacher guides, coaches, and provides instruction as students develop a need for specific information or skills related to their study. For example, if the problem involves a study of the quality of water in a nearby river, the teacher may provide lessons on how to test water for impurities, how to use the Internet to obtain information, and how to structure a report to submit to the local authorities.

Teachers who undertake problem-based learning must have a thorough understanding of the process, knowledge of students' needs, coaching/facilitating/teaching expertise, resource awareness and acquisition, and planning know-how. Because so much of the process is of an "as-you-go" variety, the teacher is constantly aware of what is happening—on one level, thinking and working with the students and on another level thinking about the process itself and his or her role as the planner and facilitator.

How Students "Do" Problem-Based Learning

Each problem-based activity differs in its action plan. However, there is a general structure that students find helpful as they begin to study the problem (see Figure 4.3). Modifications to the structure are made for younger students and for other students who have little experience with the process.

Cooperative Learning and Problem-Based Learning

Participating in groups enables students to learn with and from one another as they collaborate, discuss, and debate.

Participating in groups enables students to learn with and from one another as they collaborate, discuss, and debate. They strengthen their problem-solving capabilities as they learn to evaluate the accuracy of information from various sources, and they hone their reasoning abilities. Interdependence creates a setting for social learning in which students rely on each other to achieve their goal—to come to some conclusion relative to the problem under study. It is not only the problem's outcome that is of educational importance but also the

Steps in Problem-Based Learning

1. Meet the problem.

Students are presented with an ill-structured problem.

2. Discuss and explore the problem.

Students spend time with the problem, discussing its relevancy and what they currently know about it. They may conduct preliminary research that will enable them to better focus and narrow the problem.

3. Define the problem statement (working hypothesis).

Students work to craft a statement or question that provides focus and direction for their work.

4. Develop criteria for successful solution of the problem.

Students think about the outcome of their study in terms of expectations for performance. This step also helps to direct their focus in terms of the quality of their endeavor and conclusions.

5. Generate questions related to the problem statement.

Brainstorming specific questions related to the problem provides further focus for study, research, and data collection.

6. Develop the action plan.

Students outline what they will do and how they will do it. Determining roles and responsibilities of group members is another planning facet.

7. Gather information (research, testing, interviews, etc.).

Each member of the study team may be assigned to collect different pieces of information, which are then brought back to the group. Analyze and synthesize information and data. Information and data are compiled and put into some usable format—outline, graphs, charts, etc.

8. Generate potential solutions to the problem.

The study group uses the compiled information to answer the questions incorporated in their study. At this point, potential solutions are discussed. Or, if no solutions are feasible, explanations are given.

9. Evaluate solutions against the criteria established.

The outcome(s) of the study is compared to the criteria that were established to determine whether the group accomplished what it set out to do.

10. Present the solution to a "real" audience (those who have knowledge of the problem and are interested in the solution).

This step lends authenticity and importance to the work of the group. Regardless of the outcome, the process and findings are shared and explained.

11. Debrief the process used to arrive at the solution.

In this reflective step students deepen their understanding of learning by discussing both successful and unsuccessful strategies used in solving the problem.

Figure 4.3   Steps in Problem-Based Learning

process of achieving it. It may well be that the quality of the outcome produced is dependent on the successful interaction of the members of the group.

Johnson and Johnson (1984) point out that using cooperation in a group setting is congruent with what students will encounter in the world of work. Embedded in problem-based learning are processes that can transfer to other problem-solving scenarios (Fogarty, Perkins, & Barell, 1992). When there are similarities in the behaviors used in school and the behaviors required in the workplace, transfer of learning is more likely to occur.

Merely assigning students to participate in a cooperative group does not guarantee that they will cooperate. Teachers must teach cooperative skills and structure a setting in which cooperation is encouraged and valued (Bellanca & Fogarty, 1991).

Tools and Resources for Learning

The success of problem-based learning as an instructional strategy is in part dependent on the teacher's knowledge of the teaching and learning resources that are available. Problem-based learning requires access to current information and comprehensive resources. Students may use the Internet to acquire information, communicate with field experts, keep track of data through a database, analyze data through computer charts and graphs, produce Web pages related to their problem, and communicate their findings and recommendations on these Web pages.

The Internet can be a valuable tool for students and teachers involved in problem-based learning, but keep in mind that the Net is constantly changing and growing. Sites that are available today may not be later. Finding new sites is part of learning to use the Internet. Most Web sites are multilevel and are appropriate for the very young to the most advanced.

PLANNING PROBLEM-BASED LEARNING

Develop the Rationale for Problem-Based Learning

A clearly stated rationale is the first step in planning for problem-based learning. Teachers who use problem-based learning must be fully aware of its philosophical underpinnings and connections to the curriculum, learning standards, and assessment. PBL is a student-centered approach. The focus is on the recognition of authentic problems and the development of problem-solving skills through independent research and cooperative team skills. Teachers who are committed to PBL recognize the need to communicate the rationale to all stakeholders so that they too will understand, accept, and support it.

What's the Problem?

The basis for problem-based learning is an authentic problem or issue that is identified by the students. The learning standards are inherent in the problem. Assessments are aligned to the learning standards and thus to the problem itself. The problem should be relevant to students and at the same time hold the potential for important learnings. As the problem is discussed, students begin to outline or define an action plan. At this stage, the teacher is a guide who encourages, questions, and prompts students.

Think Ahead to the Desired Results

The desired results involved in problem-based learning are not completely apparent as students begin their discussion of the problem. Once the problem is identified and outlined, the teacher thinks ahead to the potential learning standards and assessments that eventually may become part of the overall project. A flexible mind-set is necessary since the problem may be altered by the students, thereby changing the learning standards that are addressed in the problem.

However, there should be some game plan as to how the activities will fit the required learning standards. Students as well as the teacher have the responsibility of keeping track of what learning standards are addressed at various stages in the project.

Plan Assessments

Assessment of student learning is part of any instructional approach. In a problem-based learning approach, assessment is performance based and related to learning standards inherent in the problem solution or outcomes. Students are responsible for creating schedules and timelines, checklists, and rubrics that are integral to assessing the quality of their work. Assessment documentation related to the project helps students (and their parents) clearly understand the nature of the work and how accomplishments are assessed. The Problem-Based Learning Assessment Planner (Figure 4.4) is used to document the standards and the manner in which they are assessed.

The teacher facilitates the assessment planning process and guides students to connect the problem-solving activities to the learning standards. Observing students as they work on their problem provides the teacher with information on cooperative group interactions, meeting timeline requirements, and generally how each student holds up his or her share of the workload.

A summative or final assessment indicates how students performed as well as what they learned. The summative assessment may be a final report that explains how the problem was resolved or it may be a portfolio that contains working papers, reports, and other documentation.

Plan the Teaching-Learning Design

The problem-based lesson design is not so much a lesson plan as a preliminary investigation by the teacher—a brainstorming of potential and probable ideas that may be translated into actions as students progress in their problem-based study. The type of documentation needed in PBL is more of an action plan and a summary and reflection of what occurred. This would include a description of discussion points to cover with students and the guidance they will need as they continue their projects. The teacher's role is to support, coach, and guide students toward success.

Problem-Based Learning Assessment Planner

Assessment Description

Each student group will write a report based on their study and the outcome.

1. Report is to be a group effort.
2. Report will be assessed according to the standard report rubric for this grade level.

In addition to the group report, each student is to submit a personal narrative essay describing the role he or she had in the study, problems encountered, solutions to the problems, and why the study was or was not successful.

Standards Assessed

1. Organization of information
2. Quality and depth of information
3. Use of illustrations, graphs, charts
4. Conventions
5. Presentation format
6. Personal narrative essay (written reflection)

Student Directions

- Each group is to write a report based on their study of the problem.
- Review the report-writing rubric. Be sure to address all the criteria in your report.
- Each student in the group is expected to contribute equally to the writing of the report.
- Each student will submit a personal reflection on their participation in the study and the writing of the report.
- Review the personal narrative essay rubric. Be sure to address these criteria in your reflection.

Scoring Directions

- A grade will be assigned to the group.
- An individual grade will be determined based on the personal narrative essay rubric.
- Teacher commentary based on classroom observations and ongoing assessment will be provided to each group and each student within the group. (See teacher comment sheet.)

Materials Needed

1. Report rubric
2. Personal narrative rubric
3. Teacher commentary sheet

Performance Expectations

Group reports will be evaluated according to the report-writing rubric as "Beginning," "Developing," "Developed," and "Exemplary." A Developed or Exemplary score meets expectations. Beginning and Developing level reports will receive commentary for improvement, and the group will be expected to rewrite their report.

Figure 4.4   Problem-Based Learning Assessment Planner

USING THE PROBLEM-BASED LEARNING PLANNING GUIDE

An itemized, step-by-step planning process will not fit all problem-based learning scenarios. However, a flexible structure is helpful in ensuring that important planning questions are considered. The Problem-Based Learning Instructional Design Planning Guide is a flexible structure to assist teachers in considering the important planning questions in developing a problem-based learning unit of instruction. It is composed of three sections: Section 1: Standards and Performance Descriptors—Desired Results; Section 2: Assessment—Evidence of Learning; and Section 3: Teaching-Learning Design. Each of the three sections has three columns: "Planning Questions and Decisions," "Information and Data Sources," and "Notes and Comments." The Planning Questions and Decisions column poses a series of questions to guide and stimulate thinking during the planning process. The Information and Data Sources column lists the types of resources and data sources that will facilitate answering the questions in column one. The Notes and Comments column provides information that will further clarify and assist in answering questions in column one. A detailed explanation of each section follows:

The Problem-Based Learning Planning Guide is a thinking process approach to planning instruction. The questions are a guide to specific and precise planning. Even experienced teachers with an understanding of instructional design but limited experience with PBL will find it helpful to review all the steps in the planning guide.

1. Read the Problem-Based Learning Planning Guide in its entirety.

Become thoroughly familiar with the planning guide before using it. This will save time in the long run. Get the big picture in mind before filling in the details.

2. Think it through.

Begin with Section 1: Standards and Performance Descriptors—Desired Results. Think about the questions in column one and write down thoughts and reactions. Questions may be deleted or added to accommodate specific situations. Consult the data and information sources suggested in column two and note the reminders and supplemental information in column three. Continue through Section 2: Assessment—Evidence of Learning, and Section 3: Teaching-Learning Design.

3. Synthesize the information.

Thinking through the questions on the planning guide yields a great deal of information. Teachers use this information as a touchstone as they implement the problem-based learning unit. Minilessons are designed in accordance with student needs and the learning standards that are being addressed. The format for minilessons is the Basic Lesson Plan form (the second reproducible in Chapter 1).

The Problem-Based Learning Planning Guide is shown in Figure 4.5. An example of how this guide was used by a 10th grade American history teacher is shown in Figure 4.6.

PROBLEM-BASED LEARNING PLANNING GUIDE

SECTION 1: Desired Results—Standards and Performance Descriptors

Consider these questions to plan problem-based learning.

Planning Questions and Decisions	Information and Data Sources	Notes and Comments
1. What is the advantage in using a PBL approach? Why is this approach being selected?	Review professional literature related to PBL and its effectiveness.	A clearly stated rationale conveys to all stakeholders why PBL is being used and what its advantages are in terms of student learning.
2. What "problem" topic will become the basis for this learning activity?	Conduct surveys and discuss with students their interests and concerns related to real-world problems. Students take the lead in deciding on the topic; however, the teacher determines the degree to which it fits with grade level curricula and standards.	The initial problem statement contains just enough information to elicit interest and motivation to further define the problem. The problem should have relevance to the students and be motivating. It should present some but not all information necessary to begin the study. Students must add to the information they are given so that they have a firm grasp of the problem and what they must do to solve it.
3. What learning standards are likely to be addressed through this project?	Review district and state standards, curriculum guides, and required assessments.	It is not possible to know exactly which learning standards will be involved in the problem-based learning activity at this point; however, some tentative connections will be apparent.
4. How will learning standards be organized and documented?	See the Problem-Based Learning Standards Overview (Figure 4.1) in this chapter.	Consider keeping track of standards on index cards. Pull the cards as it becomes apparent that a particular standard is addressed in students' learning. Use these standards to create assessments of student learning.

Figure 4.5   Problem-Based Learning Planning Guide

SECTION 2: Assessment—Evidence of Learning

In PBL, there is a high degree of student involvement in developing assessments. Consider these questions as a thinking guide to plan assessment of problem-based learning.

Planning Questions and Decisions	Information and Data Sources	Notes and Comments
1. How will students demonstrate their learning?	Review district and state assessments, rubrics for performance, and past practices.	The evidence of learning is through both the process of the study and the presentation of the findings. It represents the learning standards that have been covered in the problem-based study. Assessment will be ongoing and summative. Use formative assessments and observational techniques to determine student progress or difficulties.
2. Are there any embedded activities (or parts of activities) that can be used as assessments?	Student action plans will provide information related to activities and possible performance-based assessments.	The problem-based activity fits well with performance-based assessments. Students should be aware of the assessments and the criteria for performance. In most instances, they will participate in developing the criteria, rubrics, and/or checklists.
3. How will learning be reported?	Review requirements for report cards, grading scales, etc.	Consider use of student portfolios to document work throughout the project. Use rubrics to communicate standards for performance.
4. How will assessment results be used?		Use assessment results to determine student strengths and weaknesses and plan follow-up instruction. Use assessment results to communicate progress to parents and students.

Figure 4.5 (Continued)

SECTION 3: Teaching-Learning Design

Consider these questions to plan problem-based learning.

Planning Questions and Decisions	Planning Resources	Notes and Comments
1. What strategies will students use to further define the problem?		Determine how the problem will be introduced and refined. Facilitate students' exploration of the problem to enable them to verbalize (and visualize) the problem and eventually state a hypothesis.
2. What resources will students need to refine the problem statement?	Check available curriculum materials, software, Internet sites, and resource persons.	Identify possible resources and be ready to suggest and recommend them to students.
3. How will students be arranged for this initial exploration?		Determine possible grouping arrangements or procedures for self-selection of groups. Keep track of student groups.
4. How much time will be allowed for the initial exploration?	Check the school calendar and other events.	Students should be aware of the time frame and even participate in its development. It may be helpful to schedule work time on a weekly basis.
5. After the problem is refined, what strategies will students use to gather information?		Although students take the lead in what and how they will do something, the teacher needs to be prepared with procedural suggestions, recommendations, and alternatives. Students will require more support, especially when this approach is new to them, or the students are very young.
6. Identify the learning standards that are met through the problem-based study.	Review district and state standards, curriculum guides, and required courses of study.	The nature of problem-based learning makes it difficult if not impossible to connect the problem-based activities to all learning standards before the study is begun. The teacher must analyze the problem-based activity at various points along the way to account for the learning standards being addressed. Documentation of the learning standards is an important accountability measure in problem-based learning.

Figure 4.5 (Continued)

SECTION 3: Teaching-Learning Design (Continued)		
Planning Questions and Decisions	**Planning Resources**	**Notes and Comments**
7. On an ongoing basis, identify student needs related to skills, processes, and information needed to successfully participate in the problem-based activity.	Observation of students as they work and other informal assessments are used to determine needs. Refer to Basic Instructional Design, Chapter 1.	Develop lessons on content, skills, and processes as necessary. For each lesson, • Connect the purpose of the lesson to the problem. Students should understand the relevance of the lesson. • Determine how to present the lesson. • Determine what teaching-learning strategies will be most effective. • Determine what materials are needed to enhance learning. • Determine how students will be grouped for the lesson. • Determine a summarizing, reflective activity that once again connects to the problem.
8. How will students gather data and analyze potential solutions?		Be prepared with procedural recommendations for assistance when needed.
9. What are the foreseeable pitfalls?		Think ahead to what problems may occur as students begin to study the problem.
10. What alternatives (options) are available if the activity does not work out?		Involve students in evaluating their ongoing progress and determining alternatives to improve the group's work.

Figure 4.5 (Continued)

SAMPLE PROBLEM-BASED LEARNING PLANNING GUIDE FROM GRADE 10 AMERICAN HISTORY

SECTION 1: Desired Results—Standards and Performance Descriptors

Planning Questions and Decisions

1. What is the advantage in using a PBL approach? Why is this approach being selected?

I've been a teacher for 16 years. I've seen programs come and go. I haven't changed my teaching much, but lately I've realized that my students are becoming more complacent and disinterested than ever before. I did some reading on problem-based learning, and I think there may be something to it. I'm ready to try something new. I'd like my students to get more involved and interested. (I guess I'd like the same thing for myself.) My rationale for using problem-based learning is that it fits with constructivist theory and brain-based learning. It has been used in other schools with a high degree of success. There's at least enough to support it to allow for a "pilot."

2. What "problem" topic will become the basis for this learning activity?

The topic will be roots and origins of racial discrimination.
(Students will work in groups of five. Each group will work on the same problem. At the conclusion of the project, we will compare and contrast the actions and reports generated by each of the groups.)

3. What learning standards are likely to be addressed through this project?

Standards related to the problem-solving process:

    a. Identify the problem and structure a problem statement.

    b. Develop an action plan.

    c. Formulate criteria for assessing the degree of success of the task force outcomes.

    d. Collect data.

    e. Research legislation related to racial discrimination.

    f. Analyze data.

    g. Assess accuracy of information (data).

    h. Draw conclusions (formulate solutions).

    i. Write a report.

4. How will learning standards be organized and documented?

I have a list of the standards for my American History class that I can check off if I see it fits the PBL project. The report-writing rubric is already in place and reflects the district's required standards. Both these documents will be a starting point.

Figure 4.6   Sample Problem-Based Learning Planning Guide From Grade 10 American History

SECTION 2: Assessment—Evidence of Learning

1. How will students demonstrate their learning?	2. How will the assessment be scored?	3. How will the assessment be reported?	4. How will the assessment results be used?
Active participation in group activities	Teacher observation according to rubric (list of requirements and expectations)	Rubric with teacher comments will be given to each student midway through the project and at the end. Final rubric will be placed in the student's individual project file.	Feedback to students and teacher on group participation.
Selected-response test on history and origins of racial discrimination	Scoring key	Papers returned to students to place in their project file.	Feedback to students, teacher, and parents on knowledge related to racial discrimination. Scores will be included in student's quarterly grade.
Written report (group)	Rubric	Teacher conference with each group. Return a copy of the group rubric to each student in the group to be placed in their project file.	Feedback to students, teacher, and parents on final project.
Reflection paper to be completed in one class period on the following: a. The five most important things I learned in this project b. Why they are important c. How my thinking has changed d. How I feel about the project	General completion rubric: Level 1: Limited responses (1 to 4 points) Level 2: Satisfactory responses (5 to 7 points) Level 3: Extensive responses (8 to 10 points)	Papers placed in individual project file.	A summary/conclusion to the project.
Cumulative assessment based on items above	Participation: 10 points Test: 20 points Group report: 10 points Reflection: 10 points	Score sheet will be compiled and returned to students. An average composite score will be calculated.	Feedback on project. Composite scores will be included in the student's final grade.

Figure 4.6 (Continued)

SECTION 3: Teaching-Learning Design

Planning Questions and Decisions

1. What strategies will students use to further define the problem?

Students will discuss the initial problem statement and determine what information they have and what they need to determine. They will develop a more precise written statement of the problem. Main strategies will be discussion brainstorming, categorizing, and condensing.

2. What resources will students need to refine the problem statement?

Students will have access to the Internet for newspaper articles, editorials, legislation, and other related information. They may bring in any information or resources from other sources.

3. How will students be arranged for this initial exploration?

Students will work in groups of five. I will assign students to groups to attempt a good mix of personalities and cognitive levels.

4. How much time will be allowed for the initial exploration?

Two or three class periods, with out-of-class time to obtain data.

5. After the problem is refined, what strategies will students use to gather information?

I may invite some colleagues to role-play the officers, young men, mothers, etc. Students will be able to interview them to get further information on the incident.

I will have some documents on similar events for them to read.

They will use the Internet and library resources.

I may invite a judge or lawyer to talk with them about discrimination law.

6. Identify the learning standards that are met through the problem-based study.

After students begin their study, I will finalize and document the learning objectives that I listed in section one of this plan.

7. On an ongoing basis, identify student needs related to skills, processes, and information needed to successfully participate in the problem-based activity.

Minilessons will be developed for (a) how to develop an action plan, (b) keeping track of research notes, (c) racial discrimination and the law, (d) historical origins of racial discrimination, and (e) report requirements

8. How will students gather data and analyze potential solutions?

Students will work in their groups to discuss data, brainstorm, rationalize, validate, and prioritize solutions. I will work with the groups as they go through this process.

9. What are the foreseeable pitfalls?

Students don't do their part. Lack of understanding of the project and lack of commitment. I need to keep students on track.

10. What alternatives (options) are available if the activity does not work out?

Involve students in discussing alternatives. If this doesn't work, I would go back to a direct teaching model with the class as a whole instead of using the small-group structure.

Figure 4.6 (Continued)

SUMMARY OF GENERAL PLANNING STEPS FOR PROBLEM-BASED LEARNING

The steps in planning problem-based learning appear to be simple, but do not be misled. It is an ongoing, complex process that depends on the direction and focus taken by the students. On-the-spot teaching of minilessons and the flexibility to change direction are hallmarks of problem-based learning. With this in mind, the planning steps may be summarized as follows:

1. Determine rationale for using the PBL approach.

2. Use the Problem-Based Learning Planning Guide.

3. Develop the problem.

4. Determine the learning standards and benchmarks most likely to be addressed in the activities.

5. Determine possible assessments to use.

6. Develop minilessons as needed.

REFLECTIVE PRACTICE: INNER DIALOGUE

The importance of one's metacognition throughout the planning and implementation of problem-based learning cannot be overstated. Perhaps in no other approach does the teacher think as much with the students. Being aware of one's own thinking and reasoning is just as important as being aware of the students' thinking and reasoning. Bringing one's thought processes to a conscious level through reflection and inner dialogue facilitates planning and implementation.

Merely following an outline or filling in a template is not sufficient to develop expertise in planning powerful lessons. Planning is a metacognitive, reflective process in which the teacher thinks, reflects, adjusts, redirects, and fine-tunes various planning components until a powerful lesson emerges. When reflection is an intrinsic part of the planning process and teachers take time to analyze their planning efforts, they learn through their experiences, and future planning becomes more effective and efficient. What Costa (1991) called "inner dialogue" is essential to professional growth, change, and improvement. Use the Inner Dialogue page that follows (Figure 4.7) to reflect on planning actions, attempts, and results of using the Problem-Based Learning Design. Be open-minded but skeptical. Consider pros and cons, benefits and challenges. Look beyond what was accomplished to why and how it was accomplished.

Inner Dialogue

Reflect on the planning process to deepen your understanding. Keep your notes and refer to them when you plan again.

This is what I did in the planning process.	This is what I think about it and how I might change or modify it.
Some new learning	
Some benefits	
Some challenges	

Figure 4.7   Inner Dialogue

PROBLEM-BASED LEARNING STANDARDS OVERVIEW

The Problem

Reading Standards

1.
2.
3.

Writing Standards

1.
2.
3.

Listening/Speaking Standards

1.
2.
3.

Physical Education Standards

1.
2.
3.

Science Standards

1.
2.
3.

History Standards (Social Studies)

1.
2.
3.

Fine Arts Standards

1.
2.
3.

Mathematics Standards

1.
2.
3.

PROBLEM-BASED LEARNING ASSESSMENT PLAN

Assessment Description

Standards Assessed

Student Directions

Scoring Directions

Materials Needed

Performance Expectations

PROBLEM-BASED LEARNING INSTRUCTIONAL DESIGN

Planning Questions and Decisions

Desired Results	1. What is the advantage in using a PBL approach? Why is this approach being selected?
	2. What "problem" will be selected?
	3. What learning standards are likely to be addressed through this problem?
	4. How will learning standards be organized and documented?
Assessment—Evidence of Learning	5. How will students demonstrate their learning?
	6. Are there any embedded activities (or parts of activities) that can be used as assessments?
	7. How will learning be reported?
	8. How will assessment results be used?

(Continued)

(Continued)

Teaching-Learning Design	9. What strategies will students use to further define the problem?
	10. What resources will students need to refine the problem statement?
	11. How will students be arranged for this initial exploration?
	12. How much time will be allowed for the initial exploration?
	13. After the problem is refined, what strategies will students use to gather information?

Teaching-Learning Design	14. Identify the learning standards that are likely to be met through the problem-based study.
	15. On an ongoing basis, identify student needs related to skills, processes, and information needed to successfully participate in the problem-based activity.
	16. How will students gather data and analyze potential solutions?
	17. What are the foreseeable pitfalls?
	18. What alternatives (options) are available if the activity does not work out?

Resources

PROFESSIONAL TEACHING STANDARDS

The Interstate New Teacher Assessment and Support Consortium (INTASC), which includes over 30 states and professional organizations, has defined standards for what beginning teachers should know and do as they enter the profession. The National Board for Professional Teaching Standards (NBPTS) has defined standards for advanced, accomplished teaching (www.nbpts.org). These standards are used to evaluate the performance of teachers who apply for National Board certification. Another set of professional standards is the PRAXIS Series: Professional Assessment for Beginning Teachers, which was developed for use by state and local agencies to evaluate teaching performance. This work was expanded into *Enhancing Professional Practice: A Framework for Teaching* by Charlotte Danielson (1996) to include descriptors and levels of teaching performance. Many state boards of education throughout the United States have adopted professional teaching standards that replicate the components contained in the NBPTS, INTASC, and PRAXIS standards.

Interstate New Teacher Assessment and Support Consortium

The INTASC standards address the full spectrum of effective teaching components, one of which is planning for instruction. There is a clear connection between instructional planning and each of the other INTASC standards. Since *Powerful Lesson Planning* is a book about planning, each of the INTASC standards is listed with an explanation of how it relates to instructional planning. While reviewing these explanations, the reader should be mindful that the standards incorporate more than the teacher's act of planning.

Standard 1: The teacher understands the central concepts, tools of inquiry, and structure of the disciplines taught; creates learning experiences to make them meaningful to students.

Implications for instructional planning: As the teacher plans instruction, a thorough knowledge of what is to be taught and how it is to be taught is required. The instructional activities that are planned are of interest to the students and correspond directly to the learning outcome that is intended.

Standard 2: The teacher understands how children learn and develop; provides learning opportunities that support their development.

Implications for instructional planning: In an effective instructional design, the learning concepts and the instructional activities are developmentally appropriate for the students. The lesson planned is both challenging and achievable.

Standard 3: The teacher understands how students differ in their approaches to learning; creates instructional opportunities adapted to diverse learners.

Implications for instructional planning: The instructional plan shows diversification of learning activities based on student needs. Standards for learning are consistent, but the ways in which they are achieved may differ. The selected strategies are chosen to capitalize on student interests and strengths to correct deficiencies.

Standard 4: The teacher understands and uses a variety of instructional strategies.

Implications for instructional planning: The instructional plan shows the use of motivating teaching strategies that are based on "best practices." A variety of strategies are used to keep students interested and progressing toward intended outcomes.

Standard 5: The teacher creates a learning environment that encourages positive social interaction, active engagement in learning, and self-motivation.

Implications for instructional planning: The activities in the instructional plan support and promote learning through student participation and involvement in an atmosphere of mutual respect.

Standard 6: The teacher uses knowledge of communication techniques to foster active inquiry, collaboration, and supportive interaction.

Implications for instructional planning: The instructional plan includes use of engaged learning and cooperative grouping strategies as appropriate to the learning objectives.

Standard 7: The teacher plans instruction based on knowledge of subject matter, students, the community, and curriculum goals.

Implications for instructional planning: Instruction is designed to teach important concepts, skills, and processes related to the content area or field of study. Instructional plans are developed to provide students with meaningful learning experiences within the classroom and connect to related learning opportunities within the larger community.

Standard 8: The teacher understands and uses formal and informal assessment strategies.

Implications for instructional planning: The instructional plan shows that student learning is diagnosed continually through observation and informal techniques. Periodic formal assessments are used as summative measures. Students are assessed in terms of what they know and can do related to the learning objectives. Plans show that a variety of assessment strategies are used over time. Provision is made for documentation of student progress and communication of results to students and parents.

Standard 9: The teacher reflects on teaching.

Implications for instructional planning: Instructional plans are analyzed, modified, and improved through introspection and self-evaluation.

Standard 10: The teacher fosters relationships with colleagues, parents, and agencies in the larger community.

Implications for instructional planning: Parents and the community know what students are learning and are given opportunities to collaborate and support that learning. Instructional plans are shared and explained to facilitate understanding and support of the educational program.

SOURCE: Used with the permission of the Council of Chief State School Officers.

National Board for Professional Teaching Standards

While the INTASC standards focus on the core knowledge, skills, and dispositions teachers should develop (National Commission on Teaching and America's Future, 1996), the National Board for Professional Teaching Standards (1997) focuses on accomplished teaching practices in the classroom. Instructional planning and organization for teaching and learning are inherent in each of the standards. The National Board describes the standards as follows:

1. Teachers are committed to students and their learning.

Accomplished teachers are dedicated to making knowledge accessible to all students. They act on the belief that all students can learn. They treat students equitably, recognizing the individual differences that distinguish one student from another and take account of these differences in their practice. They adjust their practice based on observation and knowledge of their students' interest, abilities, skills, knowledge, family circumstances and peer relationships.

2. Teachers know the subjects they teach and how to teach those subjects to students.

Accomplished teachers have a rich understanding of the subject(s) they teach and appreciate how knowledge in their subject is created, organized, linked to other disciplines and applied to real-world settings. While faithfully representing the collective wisdom of our culture and upholding the value of disciplinary knowledge, they also develop the critical and analytical capacities of their students.

Accomplished teachers command specialized knowledge of how to convey and reveal subject matter to students. They are aware of the preconceptions and background knowledge that students typically bring to each subject and of strategies and instructional materials that can be of assistance. They understand where difficulties are likely to arise and modify their practice accordingly. Their instructional repertoire allows them to create multiple paths to the subjects they teach, and they are adept at teaching students how to pose and solve their own problems.

3. Teachers are responsible for managing and monitoring students' learning.

Accomplished teachers create, enrich, maintain, and alter instructional settings to capture and sustain the interest of their students and to make the most effective use of time. They also are adept at engaging students and adults to assist their teaching and at enlisting their colleagues' knowledge and expertise to complement their own.

Accomplished teachers command a range of generic instructional techniques, know when each is appropriate, and can implement them as needed. They are aware of ineffectual or damaging practice as they are devoted to elegant practice.

They know how to engage groups of students to ensure a disciplined learning environment, and how to organize instruction to allow the schools' goals for students to be met. They are adept at setting norms for social interaction among students and between students and teachers. They understand how to motivate students to learn and how to maintain their interest even in the face of temporary failure. Accomplished teachers can access the progress of individual students as well as that of the class as a whole. They can employ multiple methods for measuring students' growth and understanding and can clearly explain student performance to parents.

4. Teachers think systematically about their practice and learn from experience.

Accomplished teachers are models of educated persons, exemplifying the virtues they seek to inspire in students—curiosity, tolerance, honesty, fairness, respect for diversity, and appreciation of cultural differences—and the capacities that are prerequisites for intellectual growth: the ability to reason and take multiple perspectives, to be creative and take risks, and to adopt an experimental and problem-solving orientation.

Accomplished teachers draw on their knowledge of human development, subject matter and instruction, and their understanding of their students to make principle judgments about sound practice. Their decisions are not only grounded in research and professional literature, but also in their experience. They engage in lifelong learning, which they seek to encourage in their students. Striving to strengthen their teaching, accomplished teachers critically examine their practice, seek to expand their repertoire, deepen their knowledge, sharpen their judgment, and adapt their teaching to new finds, ideas, and theories.

5. Teachers are members of communities.

Accomplished teachers contribute to the effectiveness of the school by working collaboratively with other professionals on instructional policy, curriculum development, and staff development. They can evaluate school progress and the allocation of school resources in light of their understanding of state and local educational goals. They are knowledgeable about specialized school and community resources that can be engaged for their students' benefit and are skilled at employing such resources as needed. Accomplished teachers find ways to work collaboratively and creatively with parents, engaging them productively in the work of the school.

SOURCE: Reprinted with permission from the National Board for Professional Teaching Standards, *What Teachers Should Know and Be Able to Do* (1994). All rights reserved.

The Interstate New Teacher Assessment and Support Consortium (INTASC) standards were developed by the Council of Chief State School Officers and member states. Copies may be downloaded from the Council's Website at http://www.ccsso.org.

SUMMARY OF THE STUDENT EVALUATION STANDARDS

Propriety Standards

The propriety standards help to ensure that a student evaluation will be conducted legally, ethically, and with due regard for the academic well-being of the students being evaluated as well as other people affected by the evaluation results. These standards are as follows:

P1
Service to Students
Evaluations of students should promote sound education principles, fulfillment of institutional missions, and effective student work, so that the educational needs of students, community, and society are served.

P2
Appropriate Policies and Procedures
Written policies and procedures should be developed, implemented, and made available, so that evaluations are consistent, equitable, and fair.

P3
Access to Evaluation Information
Access to a student's evaluation information should be provided but limited to the student and others with established legitimate permission to view the information, so that confidentiality is ensured and privacy protected.

P4
Treatment of Students
Students should be treated with respect in all aspects of the evaluation process, so that their dignity and opportunities for educational development are enhanced.

P5
Rights of Students
Evaluations of students should be consistent with applicable laws and with basic principles of fairness and human rights, so that students' rights and welfare are protected.

P6
Balanced Evaluation
Evaluations of students should provide information that identifies both strengths and weaknesses, so that strengths can be built upon and problem areas addressed.

P7
Conflict of Interest
Conflicts of interest should be avoided, but if present should be dealt with openly and honestly, so that they do not compromise evaluation processes and results.

Utility Standards

The utility standards help to ensure that evaluations are useful. Useful student evaluations are informative, timely, and influential. Standards that promote usefulness are as follows:

U1
Constructive Orientation
Student evaluations should be constructive, so that they result in educational decisions that are in the best interests of students.

U2
Defined Uses and Users
The uses and users of student evaluations should be specified, so that the evaluation appropriately contributes to student learning and development.

U3
Information Scope
The information collected for student evaluations should be carefully focused and sufficiently comprehensive, so that the evaluation questions can be fully answered and the needs of students addressed.

U4
Evaluator Qualifications
Teachers and others who evaluate students should have the necessary knowledge and skills so that the evaluations are carried out competently and the results can be used with confidence.

U5
Explicit Values
In planning and conducting student evaluations, teachers and others who evaluate students should determine and justify the values used to judge student performance, so that the bases for the evaluations are clear and defensible.

U6
Effective Reporting
Student evaluation reports should be clear, timely, accurate, and relevant, so that they are of use to students, their parents/guardians, and other legitimate users.

U7
Follow-up
Student evaluations should include procedures for follow-up, so that students, parents/guardians, and other legitimate users can understand the information and take appropriate follow-up actions.

Feasibility Standards

The feasibility standards help to ensure that student evaluations can be implemented as planned. Feasible evaluations are practical, diplomatic, and adequately supported. These standards are as follows:

F1
Practical Orientation
Student evaluation procedures should be practical, so that they produce the needed information in efficient, nondisruptive ways.

F2
Political Viability
Student evaluations should be planned and conducted with the anticipation of questions from students, their parents/guardians, and other legitimate users, so that their questions can be answered effectively and their cooperation obtained.

F3
Evaluation Support
Adequate time and resources should be provided for student evaluations, so that evaluations can be effectively planned, implemented, interpreted, and communicated.

Accuracy Standards

The accuracy standards help to ensure that a student evaluation will produce sound information about a student's learning and performance. Sound information leads to valid interpretations, justifiable conclusions, and appropriate follow-up. These standards are as follows:

A1
Validity Orientation
Student evaluation should be developed and implemented, so that the interpretations made about the performance of a student are valid and not open to misinterpretation.

A2
Justified Conclusions
The evaluative conclusions about students' performances should be explicitly justified, so that the students, their parents/guardians, and others can have confidence in them.

A3
Defined Expectations for Students
The performance expectations for students should be clearly defined, so that evaluation results are defensible and meaningful.

A4
Context Analysis
Student and contextual variables that influence performance should be identified and considered, so that each student's performance can be validly interpreted.

A5
Documented Procedures
The procedures for evaluating students, both planned and actual, should be described, so that they can be explained and justified.

A6
Defensible Information
The adequacy of information gathered should be ensured, so that good decisions are possible and can be defended/justified.

A7
Reliable Information
Evaluation procedures should be chosen or developed and implemented, so that they provide reliable information for decisions about the performance of a student.

A8

Handling Information and Quality Control

The information collected, processed, and reported about students should be systematically reviewed, corrected as appropriate, and kept secure, so that accurate judgments can be made.

A9

Analysis of Quantitative Information

Quantitative information from student evaluations should be systematically and accurately analyzed, so that the purposes and the uses of the evaluation are effectively served.

A10

Analysis of Qualitative Information

Qualitative information from student evaluations should be systematically and accurately analyzed, so that the purposes and the uses of the evaluation are effectively served.

A11

Bias Identification and Management

Student evaluations should be free from bias, so that conclusions can be fair.

A12

Metaevaluation

Student evaluation procedures should be examined periodically using these and other pertinent standards, so that mistakes are prevented, or detected and promptly corrected, and sound student evaluation practices are developed over time.

SOURCE: Gullickson, A. R., *Student Evaluation Standards: How to Improve Evaluation of Students* (2003). Reprinted by permission of Corwin Press.

WEB SITES OF PROFESSIONAL ORGANIZATIONS

- English Language Arts

  Project of the National Council of Teachers of English (NCTE) and International Reading Association (IRA)

  www.ncte.org

- Mathematics

  National Council of Teachers of Mathematics (NCTM)

  http://standards .nctm.org

- Science

  National Science Teachers' Association (NSTA)

  www.nsta.org

- Social Studies

  National Council of Social Studies (NCSS)

  www.ncss.org

- Fine Arts

  Project of the Consortium of National Arts Education Associations (under the guidance of the National Committee for Standards in the Arts)

  www.education-world.com/standards/national/arts/index.shtml

  http://artsedge.kennedy-center.org/teach/standards.cfm

Bibliography

Allington, R. L. (1991). Effective literacy instruction for at-risk children. In M. Knapp & P. Shields (Eds.), *Better schooling for the children of poverty: Alternatives to conventional wisdom* (pp. 9–30). Berkeley, CA: McCutcheon.

Aspy, D., Aspy, C., & Quinby, P. (1993). What doctors can teach teachers about problem-based learning. *Educational Leadership, 50*(7), 22–24.

Barth, R. (1990). *Improving schools from within.* San Francisco: Jossey-Bass.

Beane, J. A. (1993). Problems and possibilities for an integrative curriculum. In R. Fogarty (Ed.), *Integrating the curricula* (pp. 69–83). Arlington Heights, IL: SkyLight Training.

Bellanca, J. (1995). *Designing professional development for change: A systematic approach.* Arlington Heights, IL: SkyLight Training.

Bellanca, J., & Fogarty, R. (1991). *Blueprints for thinking in the cooperative classroom.* Arlington Heights, IL: SkyLight Training.

Blachowicz, C., & Ogle, D. (2001). *Reading comprehension: Strategies for independent learners.* New York: Guilford Press.

Bloom, B. (1984). *Taxonomy of educational objectives: Handbook of the cognitive domain.* New York: Longman.

Brooks, J. G., & Brooks, M. G. (1993). *In search of understanding: The case for constructivist classrooms.* Alexandria, VA: ASCD.

Brophy, J., & Alleman, J. (1991). A caveat: Curriculum integration isn't always a good idea. *Educational Leadership, 49*(2), 66–70.

Burke, K. (1997). *Designing professional portfolios for change.* Arlington Heights, IL: SkyLight Training.

Burke, K. (2005). *How to assess authentic learning.* Arlington Heights, IL: SkyLight Training.

Caine, R., & Caine, G. (1991). *Making connections: Teaching and the human brain.* Alexandria, VA: ASCD.

Canady, R., & Rettig, M. (1995). The power of innovative scheduling. *Educational Leadership, 53*(3), 4–10.

Chapman, C. (1993). *If the shoe fits . . . : How to develop multiple intelligences in the classroom.* Arlington Heights, IL: SkyLight Training.

Checkley, K. (1997, Summer). Problem-based learning: The search for solutions to life's messy problems. *Curriculum Update.* Alexandria, VA: ASCD.

Costa, A. (1991). *The school as a home for the mind.* Arlington Heights, IL: SkyLight Training.

Costa, A., & Garmston, R. (1994). *Cognitive coaching: A foundation for renaissance schools.* Norwood, MA: Christopher-Gordon.

Council of Chief State School Officers. (1992). Model standards for beginning teacher licensing, assessment, and development: A resource for state dialogue. Washington, DC: Author. Http://.ccsso.org/contentpdfs/corestrd.pdf

Csikszentmihalyi, M. (1990). *Flow: The psychology of optimal experience.* New York: HarperCollins.

Cummings, C. (1980). *Teaching makes a difference.* Edmonds, WA: Teaching.

Danielson, C. (1996). *Enhancing professional practice: A framework for teaching.* Alexandria, VA: ASCD.

Darling-Hammond, L. (1997). *The right to learn.* San Francisco: Jossey-Bass.

Delisle, R. (1997). *How to use problem-based learning in the classroom.* Alexandria, VA: ASCD.

Dewey, J. (1913). *Interest and effort in education.* Boston: Houghton Mifflin.

Diamond, M., & Hopson, J. (1998). *Magic trees of the mind.* New York: Penguin Putnam.

Diller, D. (2003). *Literacy work stations: Making centers work.* Portland, ME: Stenhouse.

Diller, D. (2005). *Practice with purpose: Literacy work stations for grades 3–6.* Portland, ME: Stenhouse.

Drake, S. M. (1993). *Planning integrated curriculum.* Alexandria, VA: ASCD.

Ellis, A. K., & Fouts, J. T. (1997). *Research on educational innovations.* Larchmont, NY: Eye on Education.

Fogarty, R. (1991). *How to integrate the curricula.* Arlington Heights, IL: SkyLight Training.

Fogarty, R. (1996). *Block scheduling: A collection of articles.* Arlington Heights, IL: SkyLight Training.

Fogarty, R. (1997). *Brain compatible classrooms.* Arlington Heights, IL: SkyLight Training.

Fogarty, R., Perkins, D., & Barell, J. (1992). *How to teach for transfer.* Arlington Heights, IL: SkyLight Training.

Gandal, M., & McGiffert, L. (2003). The power of testing. *Educational Leadership, 60*(5), 39–42.

Gardner, H. (1983). *Frames of mind.* New York: Basic Books.

Gavelek, J. R., Raphael, T. E., Biondo, S. M., & Wang, D. (2000). Integrated literacy instruction. In M. Kamil, P. Mosenthal, P. D. Pearson, & R. Barr (Eds.), *Handbook of reading research* (Vol. 3, pp. 587–607). Mahwah, NJ: Erlbaum.

Gehrke, N. J. (1993). Explorations of teachers' development of integrative curriculums. In R. Fogerty (Ed.), *Integrating the curricula* (pp. 167–180). Arlington Heights, IL: SkyLight Training.

Goleman, D. (1995). *Emotional intelligence.* New York: Bantam.

Good, T., & Brophy, J. (1997). *Looking in classrooms.* New York: Addison Wesley Longman.

Goodman, Y., & Goodman, K. (1998). To err is human: Learning about language processes by analyzing miscues. In C. Weaver (Ed.), *Reconsidering a balanced approach to reading* (pp. 101–126). Urbana, IL: National Council of Teachers of English.

Guthrie, J., & McCann, A. (1997). Characteristics of classrooms that promote motivations and strategies for learning. In J. Guthrie & A. Wigfield (Eds.), *Reading engagement: Motivating readers through integrated instruction* (pp. 128–148). Newark, DE: International Reading Association.

Helm, J. (2004). Projects that power young minds. *Educational Leadership, 62*(1), 58–61.

Hunter, M. (1984). Knowing, teaching, and supervising. In P. Hosford (Ed.), *Using what we know about teaching and learning* (pp. 169–192). Alexandria, VA: ASCD.

Interstate New Teacher Assessment and Support Consortium. (1992). *Model standards for beginning teacher licensing and development: A resource for state dialogue.* Washington, DC: Council of Chief State School Officers. (www.ccsso.org/publications/details.cfm?PublicationID=86)

Intrator, S. (2004). The engaged classroom. *Educational Leadership, 62*(1), 20–24.

Jacobs, H. (1991a). On interdisciplinary curriculum: A conversation with Heidi Hayes Jacobs. *Educational Leadership, 49*(2), 24–26.

Jacobs, H. (1991b). Planning for curriculum integration. *Educational Leadership, 49*(2), 27–28.

Jacobs, H. (1997). *Mapping the big picture.* Alexandria, VA: ASCD.

Jensen, E. (2000). *Brain-based learning* (2nd ed.). San Diego, CA: The Brain Store.

Johnson, D., & Johnson, R. (1984). *Circles of learning.* Alexandria, VA: ASCD.

Joint Committee on Standards for Educational Evaluation. (2003). Gullickson, A. R. (Chair). The student evaluation standards: How to improve evaluations of students. Thousand Oaks, CA: Corwin Press.

Korbin, D., Abbott, E., Ellinwood, J., & Horton, D. (1993). Learning history by doing history. *Educational Leadership, 50*(7), 39–41.

Lewis, A. (1993). Getting unstuck: Curriculum as a tool of reform. In R. Fogerty (Ed.), *Integrating the curricula* (pp. 49 – 60). Arlington Heights, IL: SkyLight Training.

Marzano, R. (2003). *What works in schools: Translating research into action.* Alexandria, VA: ASCD

McTigue, J., Seif, E., & Wiggins, G. (2004). You can teach for meaning. *Educational Leadership, 62*(1), 26–30.

Moye, V. (1997). *Conditions that support transfer for change.* Arlington Heights, IL: SkyLight Training.

Nagel, N. (1999, November). Real problem solving and real learning. *ASCD Classroom Leadership Online, 3*(3).

National Board for Professional Teaching Standards. (1997). *What teachers should know and be able to do.* (www.nbpts.org/ Click on "Events, Calendar, and Resources" and then on "Resources.")

National Commission on Teaching and America's Future. (1996). *What matters most: Teaching for America's future.* New York: Teachers College, Columbia University.

National Center for Education Statistics. (2005). http://nces.ed.gov/

National Reading Panel. (2000). *Teaching children to read: An evidenced-based assessment of the scientific research literature on reading and its implications for reading instruction* (Report of the National Panel on Reading). Washington, DC: National Institute of Child Health and Human Development, National Institutes of Health.

Oakes, J. (1988). Tracking: Can schools take a different route? *NEA Today, 6,* 41–47.

Opitz, M. (1997). *Flexible grouping in reading: Practical ways to help all students become better readers.* New York: Scholastic.

Popham, W. J. (2005). *Classroom assessment: What teachers need to know.* Boston: Allyn & Bacon.

Relan, A., & Kimpston R. (1993). Curriculum integration: A critical analysis of practical and conceptual issues. In R. Fogerty (Ed.), *Integrating the curricula* (pp. 31–47). Arlington Heights, IL: SkyLight Training.

Rippa, S. A. (1988). *Education in a free society.* New York: Longman.

Rumelhart, D. E. (1982). *Shemata: The building blocks of cognition.* In J. T. Guthrie (Ed.), *Comprehension and teaching: Research reviews* (pp. 3–27). Newark, DE: International Reading Association.

Samara, J., & Curry, J. (1995). *Designing effective middle school units.* Austin, TX: Curriculum Project.

Samuels, S. J. (1994). Toward a theory of automatic information processing in reading revisited. In R. B. Ruddell, M. R. Ruddell, & H. Singer (Eds.), *Theoretical models and processes of reading* (4th ed., pp. 816–937). Newark, DE: International Reading Association.

Seifert, K. L. (1999). *Reflective thinking and professional development.* Boston: Houghton Mifflin.

Shanahan, T. (1997). Reading-writing relationships, thematic units, inquiry learning: In pursuit of effective integrated literacy instruction. *Reading Teacher, 51*(1), 12–19.

Shaywitz, S. E., & Shaywitz, B. A. (2004). Reading disability and the brain. *Educational Leadership, 61*(6), 6–11.

Sizer, T. (1999). No two are quite alike. *Educational Leadership, 57*(1), 6–11.

Skowron, J. (1990). Frameworks for reading instruction. *Illinois Reading Council Journal, 18*(1), 15–21.

Skowron, J. (2000). Standards and assessments: A box of chocolates? *Illinois Reading Council Journal, 28*(3), 30–37.

Skowron, J. (2003). *Differentiated instruction: Guided and independent learning for all students.* Oak Brook, IL: Academic Services.

Slavin, R. (1987). Ability grouping and student achievement in elementary schools: A best evidence synthesis. *Review of Educational Research, 57,* 293–336.

Sousa, D. (2005). *How the brain learns to read.* Thousand Oaks, CA: Corwin Press.

Sparks, D., & Hirsh, S. (1997). *A new vision for staff development.* Arlington, VA: ASCD.

Sparks-Langer, G., & Colton, A. (1991). Synthesis of research on teachers' reflective thinking. *Educational Leadership, 48*(6), 37–44.

Sprenger, M. (1999). *Learning and memory: The brain in action.* Alexandria, VA: ASCD.

Stepien, W., & Gallagher, S. (1993). Problem-based learning: As authentic as it gets. *Educational Leadership, 50*(7), 25–28.

Stepien, W., Gallagher, S., & Workman, D. (1993). Problem-based learning for traditional and interdisciplinary classrooms. *Journal for the Education of the Gifted, 16*(4), 338–345.

Stiggins, R., Arter, J., Chappuis, J., & Chappuis, S. (2004). *Classroom assessment for student learning: Doing it right—using it well.* Portland. OR: Assessment Training Institute.

Stigler, J. W., & Hiebert, J. (1999). *The teaching gap: Best ideas from the world's teachers for improving education in the classroom.* New York: Free Press.

Stronge, J. (2002). *Qualities of effective teachers.* Alexandria, VA: ASCD.

Sylwester, R. (1995). *A celebration of neurons: An educator's guide to the human brain.* Alexandria, VA: ASCD.

Sylwester, R. (2000). On teaching brains to think: A conversation with Robert Sylwester. *Educational Leadership, 57*(7), 72.

Tomlinson, C. (1999). *The differentiated classroom: Responding to the needs of all learners.* Alexandria, VA: ASCD.

Tomlinson, C., Callahan, C., Tomchin, C., Eiss, N., Imbeau, M., & Landrum, M. (1997). Becoming architects of communities of learning. *Exceptional Children, 63,* 269–282.

Tyler, R. (1949). *Basic principles of curriculum and instruction.* Chicago: University of Chicago Press.

Vacca, R. T. (2002). Making a difference in adolescents' school lives: Visible and invisible aspects of content area reading. In A. E. Farstrup & S. J. Samuels (Eds.), *What research has to say about reading instruction* (pp. 191–204). Newark, DE: International Reading Association.

Wellington, B. (1991). The promise of reflective practice. *Educational Leadership, 48*(6), 4–5.

Wiggins, G., & McTighe, J. (1998). *Understanding by design.* Alexandria, VA: ASCD.

Withrow, F., Long, H., & Marx, G. (1999). *Preparing schools and school systems for the 21st century.* Arlington, VA: American Association of School Administrators.

Zemelman, S., Daniels, H., & Hyde, A. (1993). *Best practice: New standards for teaching and learning in America's schools.* Portsmouth, NH: Heinemann.

Index

**CORWIN
PRESS**

The Corwin Press logo—a raven striding across an open book—represents the union of courage and learning. Corwin Press is committed to improving education for all learners by publishing books and other professional development resources for those serving the field of PreK–12 education. By providing practical, hands-on materials, Corwin Press continues to carry out the promise of its motto: **"Helping Educators Do Their Work Better."**